# A CHARTWELL-BRATT STUDENT TEXT

# Pascal Simply

## An introduction to Pascal Programming

## Doug Bell  Peter Scott

Department of Computer Science,
Sheffield Hallam University

 Chartwell-Bratt       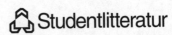 Studentlitteratur

Chartwell-Bratt (Publishing and Training) Ltd
ISBN 0-86238-368-4

Printed in Sweden
Studentlitteratur, Lund
ISBN 91-44-48571-9

Printing     1  2  3  4  5  6  7  8  9  10  |  1999  98  97  96  95  94

# Contents

Preface                                            1

1   Algorithm design                               3

2   More on algorithm design                       7

3   Some algorithm design case studies            19

4   Computers, algorithms, Pascal and all that    35

5   Pascal grammar                                 43

6   Calculations with integers                     53

7   More on procedures                             57

8   Repetition and selection in Pascal             77

9   Processing character data                      87

10  A case study in design and coding              95

11  Program layout                                103

12  Debugging and testing                         109

13  Systematic working                            115

14  Arrays                                         119

15  More on arrays                                 131

16  Real numbers                                   141

17  Top-down implementation                        147

18  File handling                                  161

Epilogue                                          169

Bibliography and further reading                  171

Syntax diagrams                                    172

# Preface

This book assumes the reader starts by knowing nothing about programming - indeed the reader need know nothing about computers. The aim is to explain the principles of programming, without getting too involved in the intricacies of a programming language. The language used is a subset of Pascal.

It is assumed that the reader has available an interactive computer facility with Pascal. The system could be a timesharing system or a micro, but the simpler and easier to use the better.

The authors strongly believe that the only way to learn about programming is to practise doing it. For these reasons, lots of problems are given for the reader to undertake. We recommend that the reader does them, as and when they are encountered, rather than skipping them and reading on.

The first three chapters of the book explain the process of program design by the method of functional decomposition - also known as top-down stepwise refinement. The notation used for design, throughout the book, is a general-purpose pseudo-code.

Top-down stepwise refinement, using pseudo-code, is the method which has been used for many years in the Computer Studies department at Sheffield City Polytechnic. It is used on *all* courses (from HNC to conversion MSc) and with *all* procedural programming languages. Design, using pseudo-code, could be studied at the same time as the reader finds out how to create files, list files, run programs and amend programs using the computer facility available.

The book goes on to explain how, in Pascal, integer numbers can be input, calculations done, and output produced. Procedures with local variables and parameters are then introduced. Next, selection and repetition are dealt with, followed by processing character data. Then comes a lull, during which no new Pascal facilities are described. Instead we examine some of the principles of systematic programming. This gives the reader plenty of time to develop the programs given as exercises, before moving onto the topics of real numbers and files. Chapters ten and onwards can be read in almost any order, depending on the interests of the reader.

The subset of Pascal used consists of:

> data types - integer, char, real, arrays
>
> control structures - procedures, if, while, for
>
> input, output - read, write of integer, char, real
>
> file handling - read, write, reset, rewrite.

The example programs used are taken from data processing, numerical computation and game playing. They are mainly interactive.

The teaching material in this book is used on a forty-hour introductory programming course on the first year of the B.Sc. in Computer Studies; but, taken at an appropriate pace, it should be suitable for students (or any other people) at *any* level.

# CHAPTER 1
# Algorithm design

## Introduction

If we wanted to construct a house we probably wouldn't start by worrying about the size of bricks. Rather we would probably think about the overall design - the layout of the house, the number of rooms and so on. Similarly, in developing a computer program we start by considering the major features of the program, rather than details like where semicolons go. This activity is called program design. For this reason, the first three chapters of this book appear to have little to do with computers or with programs. Instead they are concerned with designing programs, using a method based on algorithms.

The word "algorithm" may at first sight look like a formidable technical term. But everyone is familiar with algorithms from everyday life. An algorithm is simply a step-by-step way of doing something. For example:

1 wet hair
2 apply shampoo
3 rinse
4 repeat

Other examples of common algorithms that we see around us are: a recipe, a knitting pattern and a piece of music. The last two examples are written using special notations; the algorithms we will study use a slightly stylized form of English.

We shall see later that, in general, algorithms involve a combination of:
  a sequence of steps
  repetition
  a choice of actions.

We will write an algorithm for describing what a computer does in a special language called *pseudo-code* or *program design language* (PDL). This language looks very much like English.

An example of an algorithm written in pseudo-code is:

```
while there is more information do
     input some information
endwhile
stop
```

Looking ahead somewhat, the structures involved in an algorithm are:

### sequence
English imperative statements, doing one thing after another.

### procedure
a mini-algorithm, that is a part of a bigger algorithm.

### selection
choice of action depending on a comparison or test. This uses the if...then...else... statement.

### repetition
Doing the same thing over and over again. There are two statements to use here - while... do... and for... do...

## Algorithms involving sequences

We start by studying the simplest kind of algorithm. It involves a sequence of steps. Here is an example:

```
convert Centigrade to Fahrenheit

     multiply number by 9
     divide by 5
     add 32
```

The essential characteristic of an algorithm like this is that we start at the first instruction and obey the steps one after another in strict sequence. There is one pseudo-code instruction per line, and each instruction starts with a verb.

Here is another example:

---

```
make a cup of tea

    boil water
    warm pot
    put tea in pot
    put water in pot
    wait 2 minutes
    put milk in cup
    pour tea in cup
```
پولر قو خلا می

---

It may seem an obvious remark to say that the steps in an algorithm have to be carried out one after another. In contrast, however, you may sometimes encounter algorithms in which two or more things are done *at the same time*. This is not true of the algorithms in this book.

# Procedures

The above algorithm looks complete and unambiguous. Just as important, the steps are in the correct order. But if we gave this algorithm to someone and asked them to make a cup of tea, they might well ask for more detailed instructions. For example, they might ask what steps are involved in boiling the water. To solve this problem, we could take one of the statements and refine it - write an algorithm describing the details of the steps involved. For example, we could take "boil water" and write down the algorithm for carrying out this task:

---

```
boil water

    fill kettle
    switch on power
    wait until it boils
```

---

Similarly, we could do the same thing for any of the other steps that require amplification.

We call "boil water" a *procedure*. An algorithm is often expressed in terms of a number of procedures. These procedures may in turn involve other procedures. For example, "fill kettle" may necessitate a series of actions. When we want someone or something to obey a procedure we simply write down its name as a step within an algorithm. When we define a procedure, we write its name, followed by whatever steps it involves.

There is an important distinction to be made here. During *design*, we concentrate our attention on either the main algorithm or on a particular procedure, writing down the steps involved. Only later, when we have completed the algorithm, do we turn our attention to the details of any procedures it uses. Thus (in design) we are concerned only with *what* the procedures being used by the procedure being written do - not *how* they do it. This is a considerable aid in making sure that algorithms are easy to understand. In contrast, if we are *obeying* an algorithm, whenever we encounter the use of a procedure, we go off and do whatever steps are involved in it, returning to the step after the one that used the procedure.

## Summary

An algorithm is a set of instructions for carrying out a task. In this book, algorithms will be written in a modified form of English called pseudo-code. The simplest type of algorithm involves only a *sequence* of steps. Each pseudo-code instruction specifies an action. Often it is clearer to write an algorithm as a few, major steps. Next, any of the steps that need to be described in more detail are written down as procedures.

## Exercises

1.  Write algorithms involving sequences and procedures to:
    a.  go to work
    b.  convert a length measured in feet and inches into centimeters
    c.  make an automatic washing machine wash some clothes.

2.  Using the computer that is available to you, find out how to do the following:
    a.  correct mistakes that you make when using the keyboard
    b.  display the contents of a file
    c.  find out what files are stored in the computer
    d.  run a program that has already been written.

# CHAPTER 2
# More on algorithm design

## Selection

Some algorithms need selection - a choice of actions depending on a comparison or test. Here is an example:

```
get up
if it is a weekday then
     shave
endif
eat breakfast
```

This is a sequence of three actions: the first is "get up" and the last is "eat breakfast"; the middle action is the one that involves the selection. If it is a weekday, the person obeying the algorithm has to shave, if it is not a weekday he or she does not have to shave. Note the wording of the *if* statement. The "if", "then" and "endif" are parts of one of pseudo-code's methods of expressing selection. The words between *if* and *then*, that is "it is a weekday", specify a condition; if the condition is met then the action or actions between *then* and *endif* are to be obeyed. In this case the action is a single one - shave.

Note the layout of the selection. The *if* is written the same distance from the left-hand margin as the "get up" and "eat breakfast" because they are all parts of a sequence of actions. The "shave" is indented, or set in from the left-hand margin, because its execution is controlled by the condition immediately preceding it. It is not actually *wrong* to use any other layout, but we believe this style is the clearest.

You may have wondered what should a woman do if she had to obey the above algorithm. It is important to note that she would still have to shave; we can not

7

assume that whoever (or whatever) obeys the algorithm has any intelligence or powers of discretion; if the algorithm is wrong it will still be followed blindly.

In an *if* statement it is possible to specify several conditions rather than one, and it is possible to specify a sequence of actions rather than a single action. Here is an example which illustrates both these points:

```
get up
if it is a weekday
    and you don't cultivate a beard
    and you have stubble on your chin
then
      find a razor
      shave
endif
eat breakfast
```

Here there are three conditions: "it is a weekday", "you don't cultivate a beard" and "you have stubble on your chin". If all the conditions apply then the actions "find a razor" and "shave" should be performed.

Note that the extra conditions have been indented to allow the *if* to stand out in the text. Note also that the actions in the *then* part are indented by the same amount as each other. The placing of *then* is slightly different compared with the previous algorithm; instead of being tucked away at the end of a line, it is on a line by itself, lined up with the *if* to visually separate the actions from the conditions.

There is another kind of *if* statement that allows us to specify alternative actions. Here is an example:

```
get up
if you are male then
      shave
else
      make-up
endif
eat breakfast
```

Here we have specified an action, "shave" and a condition, "you are male"; however, we have also specified an alternative action "make-up". The alternative action is only to be performed if the condition does *not* apply. Each time the algorithm is obeyed, only one of the actions will be performed.

We can refine algorithms using procedures, just as we did with the earlier examples concerning sequences. For example:

---

Determine pension rights

```
if age > 60 then
     calculate pension payable
endif
```

---

This says that since only people over 60 are eligible for a pension, the calculation of a person's pension should only be performed if the person's age is greater than 60; if the person is 60 or less, then no action is necessary.

The next stage in developing the algorithm would be to refine the *then* part of the algorithm. For example:

---

calculate pension payable

```
if sex is female then
     calculate woman's pension
else
     check for man's pension
endif
```

---

This says that if the person is female, the pension should be calculated; if the person is male we must check to see if he is eligible for a pension.

Next it is necessary to refine the *else* part of the above procedure. This gives:

---

check for man's pension

```
if age > 65 then
     pay man's pension
endif
```

---

The above procedure takes into account the fact that men do not receive a pension until they are over 65.

There is often more than one correct algorithm for doing a particular task, and determining pension rights is no exception. Here is an alternative algorithm:

---

Determine pension rights

```
    if sex is female then
        check for woman's pension
    else
        check for man's pension
    endif
```

check for woman's pension

```
    if age > 60 then
        pay woman's pension
    endif
```

check for man's pension

```
    if age > 65 then
        pay man's pension
    endif
```

---

There is a slight problem with both the above algorithms for determining pension rights: nothing actually happens with people who are not old enough for a pension. It would be a useful exercise for you to alter them so that the user is informed when no pension is payable.

## Repetition

There are two facilities for doing repetition - the *while* and *for* statements. Here is an example that uses *while*:

---

```
open packet of biscuits
while there is a biscuit left do
    take a biscuit
    eat biscuit
    wipe up crumbs
endwhile
throw away packet
```

---

This is a sequence of three actions: the first is "open packet of biscuits" and the last is "throw away packet"; the middle action is the one that involves repetition. The "while", "do" and "endwhile" are the special pseudo-code words which are used as part of the *while* statement. The words between *while* and *do* are a condition. The words between *do* and *endwhile* are actions known as the body of the loop.

10

Note the layout of the *while* statement. The first line is aligned with the rest of the sequence of which the whole *while* statement is a part. The body of the loop is indented to show that its execution is controlled by the condition in the immediately preceding *while*.

The execution of a *while* is as follows. If the condition applies, the actions in the body of the loop are obeyed. Whenever the body has been obeyed, the condition is checked again and the actions are performed again if necessary. When the condition is no longer met, the instructions after the *endwhile* are performed. Two important points must be noted: firstly, once the condition has been tested and met, all the actions in the body of the loop will be obeyed from first to last before the condition is checked again: the condition is not rechecked after every single action; secondly, the actions in the body of the loop must be such that they eventually change the state of something involved in the condition so that it is no longer true, otherwise the algorithm would never end.

Does the algorithm work with an empty packet? Yes - the first action is obeyed, that is the packet is opened; then, if there are no biscuits in the packet, the condition is immediately untrue, so the body of the loop is skipped and the next action is to throw away the packet.

As with *if*, it is possible to have more than one condition in a *while* statement. Here is an example:

```
open packet of biscuits
while there is a biscuit left
    and you are still hungry
do
      take a biscuit
      eat biscuit
      wipe up crumbs
endwhile
put packet down
```

The *do* has been used to visually separate the conditions from the body of the loop. Alternatively we could have written both conditions on one line as follows:

```
open packet of biscuits
while there is a biscuit left and you are still hungry do
      take a biscuit
      eat biscuit
      wipe up crumbs
endwhile
put packet down
```

They both mean exactly the same. Which, if either, do you think is clearer?

Here is another example of the *while* statement:

```
set total to zero
while there is another number do
     add the number to the total
endwhile
```

This adds as many numbers as are supplied, one at a time, to a total.

Adding a few statements to the previous algorithm transforms it into this:

```
set count to zero
set total to zero
while there is another number do
     add 1 to count
     add the number to the total
endwhile
calculate average
```

The algorithm calculates the total as before; in addition, it counts the number of numbers so that an average can be calculated. It is assumed that whoever obeys the algorithm knows how to calculate an average from the total and the count; if the assumption is not valid then a refinement of "calculate average" will be needed.

## For

Here is an example of the use of the other repetition statement:

```
Live one month

     for week = 1 to 4 do
          live one week
     endfor
```

The "for", "do" and "endfor" are the special pseudo-code words which make up the *for* statement. The words between *for* and *do* specify the number of times the body of the loop is to be obeyed. The words between *do* and *endfor* make up the body of the loop.

Logically the algorithm is equivalent to this:

```
Live one month

     live one week
     live one week
     live one week
     live one week
```

The former is, however, more maintainable: it could easily be altered to cater for a different number of weeks. It is clearer: it is easier to understand "1 to 4" than it is to count occurrences of "live one week" in the second version.

As before, we can refine the algorithm further using a procedure:

Live one week

```
    for day = 1 to 5 do
        go to work
    endfor
    stay at home
    go fishing
```

The algorithm now specifies the details of how the individual days of the week should be passed.

Here is a different example:

Add up 20 numbers

```
    make total zero
    for count = 1 to 20 do
        get a number
        add number to total
    endfor
```

As written, this algorithm is a bit inflexible: it can only be used if there are 20 numbers to add up. The following is more useful:

Add up any number of numbers

```
    find out how many numbers
    make total zero
    for count = 1 to number of numbers do
        get a number
        add number to total
    endfor
```

By inserting the extra statement and changing the first line of the *for* statement, the algorithm has been made to add up lists of numbers of any length. If there turn out to be 14 numbers, the *for* statement is effectively:

```
for count = 1 to 14
```

and the body of the loop is obeyed 14 times.

Finally here is an example that uses both a *while* and an *if*. The problem is this: A bank keeps a list of customers. Each customer's entry in the list contains: the

13

account number, the current balance and the customer's name and address. We have to write an algorithm to find all customers who are overdrawn. Here is a solution:

Find overdrawn customers

```
    start at the first entry in the list of customers
    while there is an entry to check do
        check the entry
        move to the next entry in the list
    endwhile
```

Refining the statement in the body of the loop gives:

Check the entry

```
    if balance < 0 then
        write down name and address
    endif
```

# Decisions, decisions

Often when refining an algorithm several possible solutions may present themselves. For example if we have to calculate the landing time of a balloon given its launch time (in hours minutes and seconds) and flight duration (in seconds), we might come up with at least three alternative top-level algorithms.

```
convert launch time to seconds
add flight duration to give landing time in seconds
convert landing time back to hours, minutes and seconds
```

```
convert flight duration to hours, minutes and seconds
add launch and duration in hours, minutes and seconds
    to give landing time
```

```
add duration to seconds of launch time
if seconds > 59 then
    adjust seconds and minutes
    if minutes > 59 then
        adjust minutes and hours
    endif
endif
```

Our problem now is: how do we choose between these three equally correct algorithms? There is no easy answer. What we must do is refine the steps that need refining in *all three* possibilities, until we can see that one of them is wrong, or unclear or too complicated. Then, we throw that one away and continue in the same manner with the remaining two, until one of them can also be discarded. The remaining alternative is the best one.

## Level of detail

A problem when we are writing algorithms for people to obey is knowing which steps need to be refined (as procedures) and which do not. When we come to write programs, we will have no such problem; we will aim to have enough detail in our algorithms so that each step can be converted into one or two statements of a programming language. For the present, we have to make assumptions about the level of ability of the person who will obey the algorithm.

## Summary

We call

English + procedures + *while* + *for* + *if*

a program design language or pseudo-code.

The *if* statement is used to express selection.

The *while* statement can be used to repeat something zero or more times.

The *for* statement is used when we want to repeat something a known number of times.

Procedures are important because they allow us to postpone thinking about details. We can refine or fill in the details of a procedure later.

# Problems on algorithm development

Now *you* do some algorithms from the set of problems below. Forget any ideas you may have about computers and write the algorithms for people to obey. Where the problem asks for an algorithm for a machine, such as a digital watch, assume that the algorithm will be executed by one of the gremlins who live inside all such machines and are responsible for making them work. Solutions to some of the problems are given in the next chapter but don't look at our algorithms until you've had a good try at the problem.

## Selection

Write algorithms to:

1.  Calculate the net income after tax, given the following: The first 1000 pounds are tax free. Any amount earned over 1000 pounds and up to 2000 is taxed at 30%. Any amount earned over 2000 pounds is taxed at 70%.

2.  Three boxes are labelled A,B,C and each holds an unknown number of marbles. The fourth box, box D, is empty. Find the box with the largest number of marbles in it and move its marbles into box D. The operations available to you are:
    (a) compare the number of marbles in any 2 boxes
    (b) move the entire contents of one box into another.

3.  Decide what time to get up in the morning, depending on what day of the week it is.

4.  Dispense drinks from an automatic drinks dispensing machine.

## Repetition - while

Write algorithms to:

1.  Count the number of terms needed to reach a value of 1.95 when the the series  $1 + 1/2 + 1/4 + 1/8 + 1/16$  ... is added up

2.    Calculate the square root of any number using the following method:
      step 1    Start with initial estimates:
                 high guess = number
                 low guess = 0
      step 2    Calculate the average of the high and low guesses.
      step 3    If the average squared is greater than the number, make the high
                 guess equal to the average. If the average squared is less than the
                 number, make the low guess equal to the average.
      step 4    Repeat from step 2 until the result is accurate enough.

3.    Search a list of names and telephone numbers to find the number of someone
      whose name you know. Cater for not finding the name.

4.    Calculate the sines of the angles 0 to 90 degrees at intervals of 5 degrees.
      Assume you have available a procedure that calculates the sine of an angle
      expressed in degrees.

## Repetition - for

Write algorithms to:

1.    Walk up 6 flights of stairs. Each flight has 10 steps.

2.    Calculate the height, in meters, of a sheet of paper 0.1 mm thick, after it has
      been folded double 20 times.

3.    Calculate the compound interest on 100 pounds invested at 12% for six years.

4.    Take a pile of 720 widgets and pack them four to a carton; pack the cartons
      six to a box and pack those ten to a crate.

5.    Add up the series  1 -1/2 +1/3 -1/4 +1/5  ... until a term whose magnitude is
      smaller than 0.0001 has been included.

## General

Write algorithms to:

1.    Two hundred numbers are written down on a piece of paper in rows of 10.
      Find the sum and average of the numbers and the value of the largest number.
      Modify the algorithm so that it is capable of dealing with an unknown
      number of numbers, ending with an asterisk.

2.    Display the time on a digital watch face. Assume that the whole algorithm
      is executed automatically every second. Extend the algorithm so that it also
      displays the day of the week.

3. Count the number of words in a piece of text. Assume you are able to look at characters in the text one by one. The text ends with a word that begins with an asterisk (*).

4. Cross the road.

# CHAPTER 3
# Some algorithm design case studies

In this chapter we will write some of the algorithms suggested as exercises in the previous chapter. The first one we will study is this:

> Calculate the net income after tax, given the following: The first 1000 pounds are tax free. Any amount earned over 1000 pounds and up to 2000 is taxed at 30%. Any amount earned over 2000 pounds is taxed at 70%.

If we think about the problem, we should see that even though the problem is given under the heading "selection", the top-level solution is a *sequence* of two actions.

---
Calculate net income

```
    calculate tax payable
    take tax payable from gross income giving net income
```
---

Of these two actions, only the first needs refining. We have to decide whether or not there will be any tax to pay. This is determined by comparing the gross income with £1000.

---
calculate tax payable

```
    if gross income is £1000 or less then
        set tax payable to 0
    else
        calculate actual amount of tax
    endif
```
---

Again there is only thing to refine. Calculating the actual amount of tax depends on whether the person earns more than 2000 pounds, if they do there is one formula to apply, if not there is another. This gives:

```
calculate actual amount of tax

    if gross income is £2000 or less then
        set taxable income to gross income - £1000
        set tax payable to taxable income x 0.3
    else
        set high rate income taxable to gross income - £2000
        set high rate tax to high rate income taxable x 0.7
        set tax payable to high rate tax + £300
    endif
```

# Number of Terms in Series

Count the number of terms needed to reach a value of 1.95 when the the series $1 + 1/2 + 1/4 + 1/8 + 1/16$ ... is added up.

This problem can be done by an algorithm which has a sequence as its top level. To calculate the number of terms, we must:

```
Calculate the number of terms

    set sum to zero
    set count of terms to zero
    add in and count enough terms
    give count as answer
```

The third action is the one that needs refining. At this point, or even earlier, most books on programming and most experienced programmers would probably say, "A little reflection should show us that what is needed is this...", and then proceed to give a seven or eight line algorithm. What this means is that the author or programmer has written so many algorithms that he or she can remember a general solution to problems of this kind, and can mentally modify it to fit this case before writing it down. If we saw such a solution, we could probably understand that it did work. Unfortunately it would not tell *us* how to arrive at a working solution for ourselves.

There are at least two lines of reasoning. The following is probably the better one. First, we choose from sequence, selection and repetition, and decide that repetition will be most useful in adding enough terms. Having decided on repetition, we choose *while* rather than *for*, because we will not know, at the time the algorithm is executed, exactly how many times the body of the loop will need to be performed.

Having chosen *while*, we need to decide on a condition to use in it. This should come straight from the problem: the condition is that the sum must be less than 1.95. We can see that the condition will be met initially because of the setting of sum to zero in the top-level algorithm, so that the body of the loop will be executed at least once. This leads us to:

Add in and count enough terms

```
    while sum < 1.95 do
        ? ? ? ?
    endwhile
```

We can now consider what to put into the body of the loop. Clearly, we must add the current term into the sum and add one to the count of the number of terms. Straight away, we see that we had better ensure that we start with a term of one. Thus:

Add in and count enough terms

```
    set term to one
    while sum < 1.95 do
        add term to sum
        add one to counter
    endwhile
```

There is something missing from this. If we executed it, we should finish with a count of 2 and sum of 2. We need something in the body of the loop to calculate the next value for term. The best place is just before the *endwhile*. This gives:

Add in and count enough terms

```
    set term to one
    while sum < 1.95 do
        add term to sum
        add one to counter
        set term to half its present value
    endwhile
```

If we had put that line in just after the *while* we would have had to have changed the initial setting of term to 2. This would not have been as clear. It is better, in situations like this, to use the values and then to change them to suit the next time through the loop.

An alternative line of reasoning to arrive at the same refinement of "add in and count enough terms" is as follows. We have to do something like this:

---

Add in and count enough terms

```
    calculate the first term
    add term to sum
    add one to count
    calculate next term
```

---

We then see that the last three steps need to be repeated a number of times, so we must "wrap them up" in some form of repetition. A similar argument to the one above leads us to choose a *while* rather than a *for*. This gives:

---

Add in and count enough terms

```
    calculate the first term
    while sum < 1.95 do
         add term to sum
         add one to count
         calculate next term
    endwhile
```

---

Refining the two lines which calculate terms, and placing the final refinement in the original top-level algorithm leaves us with what the experienced programmer would have written down with little conscious thought:

---

Calculate the number of terms

```
    set sum to zero
    set count of terms to zero
    set term to one
    while sum < 1.95 do
         add term to sum
         add one to counter
         set term to half its present value
    endwhile
    give count as answer
```

---

Take heart - practice will do the same for you! In this example, we chose to present the final algorithm without using procedures, because it shows the structure of the algorithm more clearly. This is not always the case.

# Sum of series

Add up the series  1 -1/2 +1/3 -1/4 +1/5  ... until a term whose magnitude is smaller than 0.0001 has been included.

If we treat the first term of the series as 1/1, we see that the divisors follow the sequence 1, 2, 3, 4, etc. Also, there is a pattern in the signs of the terms: they are alternately positive and negative. The last divisor for the terms which must be included in the sum is 10001 since 0.0001 is 1/10000 and the specification says that a "term whose magnitude is *smaller* than 0.0001" has to be included. We should see that some sort of repetition is needed to include many terms in the sum. Since we know now how many terms will be needed, we choose a *for* rather than a *while*. When we consider the inclusion of the term in the sum, we should be reminded that we have to give sum an initial value. This gives:

Sum of series

```
    set sum to zero
    for divisor = 1 to 10001
        calculate term and include in sum
    endfor
```

Next we must refine "calculate term and include in sum". The term is clearly calculated by dividing one by the divisor. The tricky part is to ensure that terms are alternately added and subtracted. This can be done by having something called sign whose value alternates between +1 and -1. If the term is multiplied by sign before it is added to the sum, all will be correct. We will have to arrange for sign to start off with the value of +1 before the *for*. This gives:

Sum of series

```
    set sum to zero
    set sign of next term to +1
    for divisor = 1 to 10001
        calculate term and include in sum
    endfor
```

calculate term and include in sum

```
    set term to 1 divided by divisor
    add term times sign to sum
    prepare for next term
```

The only thing left to refine is "prepare for next term". All that needs to be done is to ensure that sign is changed, so that if it has a value of +1 it is changed to -1,

23

and vice versa. This could of course be done using an *if*. Alternatively, it could be done like this:

---

prepare for next term

```
        set sign to  - (sign)
```

---

If sign is +1 it becomes -(+1) which is -1. If sign is -1 it becomes -(-1) which is +1. You might argue that it would have been clearer to have used an *if*, especially as the shorter way needed so much explanation!

Because this is only one line, it is probably clearer to insert this refinement directly in "calculate term and include in sum". This leaves us with:

---

Sum of series

```
        set sum to zero
        set sign of next term to +1
        for divisor = 1 to 10001
            calculate term and include in sum
        endfor
```

calculate term and include in sum

```
        set term to 1 divided by divisor
        add term times sign to sum
        set sign to - (sign)
```

---

An alternative algorithm could be obtained if we looked at the pattern of the signs of the terms in a different way. We might notice that the terms with odd divisors are added to the sum and those with even divisors are subtracted from the sum. That reasoning leads to this algorithm:

---

Sum of series

```
        set sum to zero
        for divisor = 1 to 10001
            calculate term and include in sum
        endfor
```

calculate term and include in sum

```
        set term to 1 divided by divisor
        if divisor is odd then
            add term to sum
        else
            subtract term from sum
        endif
```

---

# Packing 720 widgets

Take a pile of 720 widgets and pack them four to a carton; pack the cartons six to a box and pack those ten to a crate.

A little arithmetic tells us that 720 widgets will occupy 180 cartons. Those 180 cartons will be packed in 30 boxes. The boxes will occupy three crates. Packing crates of widgets does seem to be a repetitive process. Since we know now, how many of each object we have to deal with, we can use *for* throughout the algorithm. This is the top level algorithm:

Pack 720 widgets

```
for crate = 1 to 3 do
     fill a crate with boxes of widgets
endfor
```

There is only one thing to refine. It looks very similar to the top level:

fill a crate with boxes of widgets

```
for box = 1 to 10 do
     fill a box with cartons of widgets
     put it in the crate
endfor
```

Doing the obvious refinements we get this algorithm:

fill a box with cartons of widgets

```
for carton = 1 to 6 do
     fill a carton with widgets
     put it in the box
endfor
```

Doing more obvious refinements we get this algorithm:

fill a carton with widgets

```
for widget= 1 to 4 do
     pick up a widget from the pile
     put it in the carton
endfor
```

Notice how the use of procedures makes a potentially complex algorithm simple.

# Cross the road

Crossing the road requires a lot of intelligence. Since we do not want to spend an inordinate amount of time on it, we will write an algorithm that will only deal with ordinary roads. If you want to cross a motorway, a dual carriageway or a one-way street, find another algorithm first! The first attempt should look like this:

<u>Cross an ordinary road</u>

```
wait on the pavement as long as the road is not clear
walk to the other pavement
```

The waiting is the action that needs refining. When the authors were children, they were taught to look right, look left, look right again and then to cross the road if it was clear. Those instructions are a bit ambiguous so we will try and express their spirit in pseudo-code. The tricky bit is that if at any time we notice that the road is not clear, we have to begin again with look right, look left and so on. This needs to be expressed with the *while* form of repetition. Thus:

<u>wait on the pavement as long as the road is not clear</u>

```
while we have not decided that the road is clear do
    look right, look left etc.
endwhile
```

This will do nothing except look right, look left etc., until we have decided that the road is clear. Doing nothing has the effect of leaving us on the pavement - waiting, which is what we should do.

A first attempt at refining the body of the *while* might give something like this:

<u>look right, look left etc.</u>

```
look right
if it is clear then
    look left etc.
else
    ? ? ? ? ?
endif
```

The difficult part is what to do in the *else*. The above discussion might make us want to put something there such as: "go back to looking right", "pack in" or "exit". The effect of all of those is achieved by doing nothing in the *else*. That is by using an *if* without an *else*. We do not have to worry about "going back", we took care of that part of the problem when we chose to call "look right, look left etc." from the body of a *while*. The correct refinement is:

```
    look right
    if it is clear then
        look left etc.
    endif
```

Refining the only complicated part of that gives:

look left etc.

```
    look left
    if that is also clear then
        look right (again)
    endif
```

The same kind of reasoning gives:

look right (again)

```
    look right
    if that is still clear then
        declare the road well and truly clear
    endif
```

We leave the algorithm in that form.

You may have chosen something like the following as your refinement of "look right, look left etc":

```
look right
wait until clear
look left
wait until clear
look right
wait until clear
```

This is wrong! It merely waits until there has been a gap in the traffic coming from the right, followed by one in the traffic coming from the left and another from the right. It does not ensure that the gaps from the left and right occur at the same time. In other words, it does not ensure that the road is clear.

An other way of presenting the mini-algorithm "look right, look left etc." would be to put the refinements of the various parts at the places they were first needed. The algorithm would then appear thus:

```
    look right
    if it is clear then
        look left
        if that is also clear then
            look right (again)
            if that is still clear then
                declare the road well and truly clear
            endif
        endif
    endif
```

The logic is the same as before, but we have lost the insight into the author's thought processes when he designed the algorithm. We also have an algorithm that involves a number of possibly confusing "nested" *if* statements. In other words, this presentation is slightly less clear. Do you agree?

# Search a list of names and telephone numbers

Search a list of names and telephone numbers to find the number of someone whose name you know. Cater for not finding the name.

To look up a name in a list of names, we have to start at the top of the list and run our finger (or at least our eyes) down the list until we come to the name we seek, or until we come the end of the list, whichever comes first. When we stop scanning the list, if we found the name, we can use the telephone number. The initial algorithm is therefore:

Search list of names

```
    put finger by first name in list
    scan list
    use number (if found)
```

To scan the list, we have to repeatedly move our finger to the next name in the list. To perform an action an indefinite number of times, we must enclose it in a *while*. We have to stop moving down the list when we find the name for which we are looking, or when we reach the end of the list. These two therefore are the conditions to use in the *while*. This gives:

```
scan list

    while name by finger is not the sought name
        and finger not at last name in list
    do
        move finger to next name in the list
    endwhile
```

It could be argued that the first line in the main algorithm is really just some initialisation needed to ensure that the *while* loop starts off correctly. If we accept that, the algorithm so far becomes:

```
Search list of names

    scan list
    use number (if found)

scan list

    put finger by first name in list
    while name by finger is not the sought name
        and finger not at last name in list
    do
        move finger to next name in the list
    endwhile
```

When the execution of the body of the while finishes, it can be for one of two reasons: either we have reached the name we were seeking, or we have reached the end of the list. Both may occur together; so we had better check to see if the name by the finger is the sought name, rather than check to see if we are at the end of the list. "Use number (if found)" can thus be refined as:

```
use number (if found)

    if name by finger is the sought name then
        use the telephone number
    else
        decide that the name is not listed
    endif
```

# Counting words in a piece of text

Count the number of words in a piece of text. Assume you are able to look at characters in the text one by one. The text ends with a word that begins with an asterisk (*).

To count the number of words in a piece of text, we should first set a count of the number of words to zero. Then we should count the ordinary words. Lastly we should be careful to count the last word as well as the others. The first refinement is therefore:

---

Count words

```
set number of words to zero
count ordinary words
count last word
```

---

A piece of text that contained only the special last word would have no ordinary words in it. The middle step should therefore add nothing to the count, so the algorithm would produce a count of one when executed with that text. With that reasoning, we have shown that the algorithm is correct.

Notice that the algorithm could have been shortened by setting the count to one and missing out the last step. This kind of trick is often used unconsciously in programs. It has not been used here as it leads to a reduction in clarity.

Now we have to decide how to count the ordinary words. We should scan through the text from the beginning, adding one to the count every time we encounter another word. The counting and scanning need to be executed again and again as long as the last word has not been reached. This is achieved by controlling the execution of counting and scanning with a *while*. The mini-algorithm is therefore:

---

Count ordinary words

```
put finger at start of first line of text
move finger to start of first word
while word by finger is not the last word do
     add one to number of words
     move finger to start of next word
endwhile
```

---

If there are any ordinary words in the text, the body of the while will be obeyed once for each word, giving the correct value of count.

The condition in the *while* in the preceding algorithm could be made more explicit by noting that the special end-word begins with an asterisk. Thus it is not necessary to look at the whole of the last word at once. Anyhow, we must comply with the specification which tells us to examine one character at a time. A better version of the procedure is:

---

<u>Count ordinary words</u>

```
     put finger at start of first line of text
     move finger to start of first word
     while character by finger is not an asterisk do
           add one to number of words
           move finger to start of next word
     endwhile
```

---

Next we refine "move finger to start of first word". If the text contains spaces at the start of the line, we will need to skip past them. If there are none, we do nothing. This leads to:

---

<u>move finger to start of first word</u>

```
     while character by finger is a space do
           move finger to next character position
     endwhile
```

---

Notice that there was no need to use an *if*. The *while* does nothing if the first character on the line is not a space.

Now we need to refine "move finger to start of next word", keeping in mind the fact that words may be separated by one or more spaces.

---

<u>move finger to start of next word</u>

```
     move finger to next space
     move finger past consecutive spaces
```

---

The refinement of the first of the steps is very similar to the last refinement but one:

---

<u>move finger to next space</u>

```
     while character by finger is not a space do
           move finger to next character position
     endwhile
```

---

The refinement of "move finger past consecutive spaces" is slightly more complex. It is similar to "move finger to start of first word", but instead of simply moving the finger, we must take care to move to the next line if we have reached the end of a line. When we move to the next line, the task if not necessarily over: the line may start with spaces or may contain only spaces. Thus the test for end of line should be governed by the *while*. This gives:

```
move finger past consecutive spaces

    while character by finger is a space do
         if finger is at end of line then
              move finger to start of next line
         else
              move finger to next character position
         endif
    endwhile
```

The above procedure may be used instead of "move finger to start of first word", allowing us to discard that procedure, and making our main algorithm deal with text even if it begins with blank lines. The final version of the algorithm is:

<u>Count words</u>

```
set number of words to zero
count ordinary words
count last word
```

<u>Count ordinary words</u>

```
put finger at start of first line of text
move finger past consecutive spaces
while character by finger is not an asterisk do
      add one to number of words
      move finger to start of next word
endwhile
```

<u>move finger to start of next word</u>

```
move finger to next space
move finger past consecutive spaces
```

<u>move finger to next space</u>

```
while character by finger is not a space do
      move finger to next character position
endwhile
```

<u>move finger past consecutive spaces</u>

```
while character by finger is a space do
      if finger is at end of line then
            move finger to start of next line
      else
            move finger to next character position
      endif
endwhile
```

## Summary

Designing algorithms is not easy, but step-wise refinement helps.

Understanding other people's designs is difficult, but it is less so if the designs have small procedures.

Most people need lots of practice before they become proficient at designing.

# Exercises

If you skipped the exercises in the first two chapters, go back and do them before going on!

# CHAPTER 4
# Computers, algorithms, Pascal and all that

## What is a computer?

For the purposes of this book, the hardware of a computer looks like this:

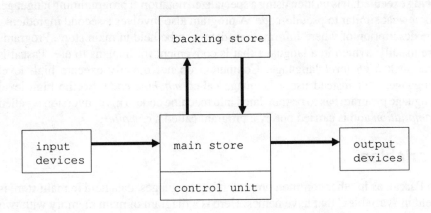

The most common input device is a terminal keyboard. Other examples are paper tape and punched card readers. The most common output device is the vdu screen. Another example is a printer. Backing store is such things as magnetic disc and tape.

# What is it that a computer can do?

First, it can hold information, numbers and text, in main store or backing store (We will discuss the use of backing store more fully in chapter 18).

Second, the control unit enables a computer to obey an algorithm that is held in main store. An algorithm for a computer involves sequences, selections and repetitions like those we have seen and used in the first three chapters. In addition the actions that are unique to a computer are that it can:

> input information from an input device into main store,
> output information from main store to an output device,
> transfer information from main store to backing store and vice versa,
> copy information from one place in main store to another, and
> do calculations on numbers held in main store.

Whether a computer is used to control a power station or play chess, the software is built from algorithms involving just these few operations.

A program consists in part of an algorithm involving these operations. The algorithm is held on backing store and is brought into main memory while it is being executed. It is written using a specialized notation, a programming language, somewhat similar to pseudo-code. A program also involves a second ingredient - the description of where information (data) can be held in main store. Programs are usually written in a language that is convenient for humans to use. Pascal is one such *high level* language. Computers do not directly execute high level languages, but instead use a language called *machine code*. So the high level language program has to be translated into machine code. This conversion is called *compilation* and is carried out by a program called a *compiler*.

# Variables

In Pascal, as in other common programming languages, data held in main store is held in "variables" that have names. Here is a diagram of main memory with two variables.

```
     age   | 27     |

telephone  | 335216 |
```

We can think of variables as being like boxes, each of which can hold a number. Each box has a name, given to it by the programmer. In the above, the box (variable) named "age" contains the value 27. Often the contents of a box will change as it is acted upon by the instructions in the program.

Here at last is a program that inputs a number from the keyboard into a variable and then outputs it to the screen:

```
program echo (input, output) ;

var   age : integer ;

begin
read (age) ;
write (age)
end.
```

Do not worry about the layout of this program, semi-colons, etc. We will sort out the details of converting algorithms to programs later.

The program begins with the language word *program* followed by whatever name we choose to give to the program. Language words are like *if* and *while* in pseudo-code - they have special meanings. Any variables are described after the language word *var*. This program uses only one variable, which the programmer has named "age". It is a variable that can be used to hold a single integer (whole) number. The word *begin* introduces the algorithmic part of the program, which consists of two steps. The first instructs the computer to input a number (an integer) from the keyboard and place its value in the variable called age. The second instructs the computer to output the value of the integer onto the screen. The word *end* followed by a period ends the algorithm and the program.

Here is a diagram that shows what this program would do:

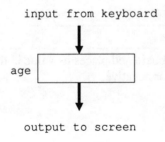

input from keyboard

age

output to screen

You could run the program to check that it actually does this !

Here is another, slightly more complex program:

```
program play (input, output) ;
var
    x, y, z : integer ;
begin
x := 42 ;
read (y) ;
z := y + 7 ;
write (z)
end.
```

Here there are now three variables, called x, y and z. The *read* and *write* statements work as before.

A new statement is:

```
x := 42
```

The ":=" should be read by us humans as "becomes". So the statement means that the value of the variable called x becomes 42. Alternatively we can interpret the statement as meaning that the value 42 is placed in the box x. This kind of statement is called an *assignment* statement because a value is assigned to (given to) a variable. Similarly

```
z := y + 7
```

means that z becomes the value of variable y plus 7. Or, calculate (y + 7) and place the answer in z.

What happens if a value of 4 is input?

## Input and Output

We have seen that the statement:

```
read (fred)
```

inputs an integer from the keyboard and places its value in the variable fred. The number can either be positive or negative.

If we need to input a set of three numbers, we might write:

```
read (first) ;
read (second) ;
read (third)
```

Alternatively, if we were feeling a little lazy, or if it seemed to be clearer, we could write:

```
read (first, second, third)
```

which is exactly equivalent.

When a program requests a series of numbers like this, they are keyed in one after the other, with one or more spaces between them. Alternatively, they can be on separate consecutive lines.

We have already seen the use of the *write* statement. If we need to output a series of values, and we want to save ourselves a little writing, we can use the *write* statement like this:

```
write (a, b, c ... )
```

to output the values of a, b, c and so on to the screen.

If we use only *write* statements to output information, the system will display them where it chooses, using spaces and new lines as necessary. In order to have greater control, we can use the instruction with the strange name *writeln*. Execution of the statement:

```
writeln
```

directs the vdu to go on to the start of the next line. For example, if a has a value of 1, b has a value of 2, and c has a value of 3, then the statements:

```
write (a,b) ;
write (c) ;
writeln
```

give the following output on the screen:

```
    1   2   3
```

But:

```
write (a,b) ;
writeln ;
write (c) ;
writeln
```

gives:

```
    1    2
    3
```

## Output of text

So far we have only output numbers to the screen. Often we want to output text consisting of letters, spaces, and other characters. To do this we simply write the text inside single quotation marks, like this:

```
program friend (input, output) ;
begin
write ('hello') ;
writeln
end.
```

If the text has to contain the single quotation mark character, we have to include two of them; like this:

```
write ('Janet''s program')
```

# Procedures

Here is a program that has some procedures in it - the usual situation.

```pascal
program add (input, output) ;

var x, y, sum : integer ;

procedure readData ;
begin
write('enter 2 numbers') ;
writeln ;
read (x, y)
end ;

procedure doCalc ;
begin
sum := x + y
end ;

procedure giveResult ;
begin
write (x) ;
write ('+') ;
write (y) ;
write ('=') ;
write (sum) ;
writeln
end ;

begin
readData ;
doCalc ;
giveResult
end.
```

Notice that procedures are declared and called in a similar way to pseudo-code. To call a procedure, simply write down its name (all one word now, though). The language word *procedure* introduces the declaration of a procedure. The algorithmic statements of a procedure are sandwiched between the language words *begin* and *end*. An inconvenient rule of Pascal requires that any procedure must be declared before it is used. So in Pascal the main program is always at the end, after the procedures. Also, a procedure which uses other procedures has to come after the procedures that it uses.

Again, do not worry about where things like semi-colons go. We will sort this out later.

# Summary

A computer is machine that will hold information (data) in memory and execute an algorithm to act upon the data. A computer program consists of two parts - an algorithm and a description of the variables. Variables are named boxes in main memory, available to hold data. We have seen how to do the following in Pascal:

1. input a number from the keyboard, placing the value in a variable.

2. output a number from a variable to the screen.

3. give a variable a definite numeric value.

4. add the contents of variables, and place the result in a variable.

5. output text.

6. call procedures.

# Exercises

1. Using your computer facility:
   a. find out how to enter a program into the computer,
   b. enter some of the programs given above,
   c. find out how to correct or alter a program that you have entered,
   d. run the program and see if it behaves as expected.

2. Alter the above programs so as to create programs that:
   a. input 3 numbers and add them together,
   b. input 3 numbers and then display them in reverse order.

# CHAPTER 5
# Pascal grammar

When we use natural languages, such as English or French, we have to be aware of the grammar of the language; it is just the same with programming languages. The main area in which we are interested in this chapter is *syntax* - the order of words and punctuation symbols in the language. (The other area which concerns us is the meaning of the programs in the language). It would be very long-winded and tedious to describe all the syntax of a language in words, so we use syntax diagrams for some parts. Many programming books and manuals usually either use these diagrams, or use another method and supply the diagrams as an appendix.

Suppose we wanted to describe correct English syntax. In particular, suppose we wanted to describe such simple sentences as:

the man owns the dog
she sees the big fat cat

We could use syntax diagrams like these:

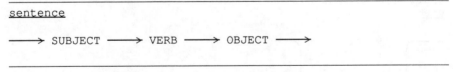

sentence

$\longrightarrow$ SUBJECT $\longrightarrow$ VERB $\longrightarrow$ OBJECT $\longrightarrow$

Syntax diagrams can be interpreted in two ways. The simplest is that the above means: a sentence consists of a subject followed by a verb followed by an object. Alternatively, we can use syntax diagrams to create or generate syntactically correct sentences. To do this we have to start at the left hand side of the diagram and follow the lines in the direction shown by the arrows, always finishing at the right-hand side. When we come to a fork, we can take any one of the branches.

When we come to uppercase words, we have to find another syntax diagram with those words as its title, use it and then return to the current diagram, resuming at the point at which we left off. When we come to anything else, we have to write it down.

Thus the above diagram also tells us that subject, verb and object are themselves defined in other syntax diagrams. These are as follows:

subject

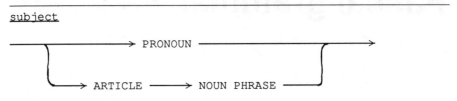

This says that the subject of a sentence is either a pronoun, or an article followed by a noun phrase, and that those three are all defined in other syntax diagrams.

noun phrase

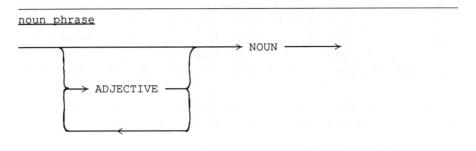

This defines a noun phrase as being zero or more adjectives followed by a noun.

verb

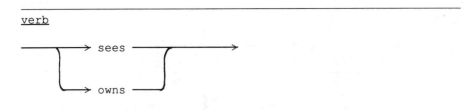

This tells us we have of choice of two verbs - sees or owns.

You draw the remaining syntax diagrams needed to complete the definition of the simple sentences we started with.

## Limitation

When you have completed the syntax diagrams, they will allow such sentences as "the dog owns the man". This is a limitation of *all* syntax descriptions: they do not take account of the *semantics* or meaning of the sentences. Thus a sentence (or program) may be syntactically correct but meaningless or wrong.

## Pascal Syntax

Here is a description of the grammar of the (subset of) Pascal that we have used so far. There will be additions and changes later.

Program

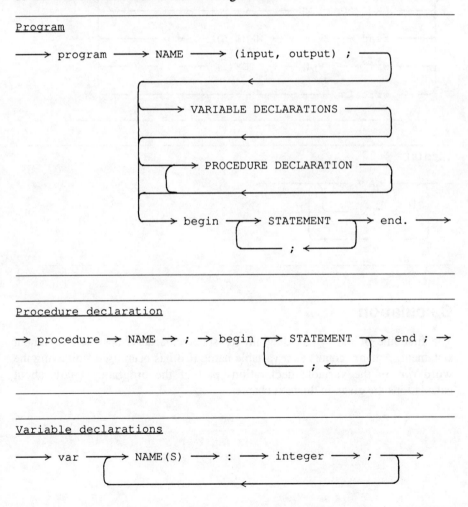

Procedure declaration

→ procedure → NAME → ; → begin ┬→ STATEMENT ┬→ end ; →
                                  └─── ; ←───┘

Variable declarations

──→ var ┬→ NAME(S) ──→ : ──→ integer ──→ ; ┬──→
         └──────────────← ──────────────────┘

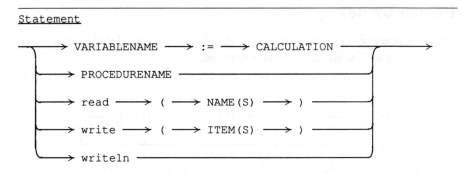

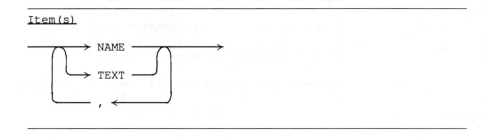

## Calculation

The first line of the syntax diagram for statements describes the assignment statement. A name counts as a variable name if it has been used, following the word *var*, in the variable declarations part of the program. Details about calculations are given in the next chapter.

## Procedurename

In Chapter Four we saw that to call a procedure in Pascal you just write the name of the procedure; this is what is meant by the "procedurename" line in the syntax diagram for statements. A name counts as a procedure name if it has been used, following the word *procedure*, in the procedure declaration part of the program. Don't forget that procedures must be declared before they can be used.

## Names

Variable names, procedure names and all other names in Pascal begin with a letter and are made up of letters and digits; they cannot contain spaces or hyphens. As an exercise, you could draw a syntax diagram to describe them.

It would be more tedious to draw syntax diagrams for letters and digits, than to describe them in English. A letter is what everyone understands by a letter: one of the symbols from 'a' to 'z' or from 'A' to 'Z'. Similarly, a digit is one of the symbols from '0' to '9'. Their syntax diagrams would have a 52-way branch and a ten-way branch respectively.

If all these syntax diagrams and rules seem overwhelming and you think you will never remember them all, take heart - you do *not* need to! There is no virtue in memorizing the rules of the grammar of a programming language. Even professional programmers do not remember all the details. To check the grammar, they usually either look at an earlier program or refer to a manual.

## Some more rules about names (sorry!)

There are some restrictions on the names you can use in Pascal. Firstly, the name must not conflict with the language words such as *begin* and *end*. These words are sometimes called *reserved words*. The manual for the computer you use will give a list of these for its version of Pascal so that you can avoid them.

Secondly, some versions of Pascal do not take all the characters into account in long names. The definition of long varies from machine to machine, but your computer will use at least the first eight characters of names. A system which restricted the length of names to eight characters would treat numberofmarbles and numberofboxes as if they were the same name. This could prevent otherwise-correct programs from working. Notice that we have to run parts of names together because names cannot include spaces.

Thirdly, some systems treat all letters as if they were capitals; which means that count and COUNT would be taken to be the same name. We have already seen that names cannot contain spaces. Because we cannot break them up with spaces, names such as numberofmarbles will be difficult to read. In this book therefore, we will write names consisting of more than one part like this - numberOfMarbles. A system which treats all letters as capitals can cause problems here as it would treat doOrPost and doorpost as if they were the same name. If your computer has any of the above limitations you will have to make whatever allowances are needed.

Finally, variable names are only recognised if they have been included in the variable declarations part of the program. This is so that the compiler can check that we have been consistent with the spelling of all our variable names.

You might notice that some of the examples which follow use one-character variable names. This is perfectly acceptable in Pascal but, as we will see later, it often leads to unclear programs. We have used them only for simplicity in abstract program fragments. We suggest that you use longer, meaningful variable names.

## Semicolons

Semicolons in Pascal are a pain in the neck. They *separate* statements rather than *terminate* them. The difference between separators and terminators is best illustrated by ordinary English sentences. In those, commas are used to separate the phrases, and a full stop is used to terminate the whole thing. So in Pascal you use semicolons between statements to indicate that there is another statement coming along next. Another way to look at it is to remember the rule that you use a semicolon after every statement *except* that you don't have one before *end* or *else*.

## Spaces and newlines

The rules about where to put spaces are much the same in Pascal as in English. At least one space is needed if a name or reserved word directly follows another name or reserved word. Wherever there is a space or punctuation symbol, it can be preceded and/or followed by any number of spaces. Hyphenation is not allowed in Pascal: a word at the end of a line is always regarded as being separate from the word at the beginning of the next line. In Pascal, spaces are not allowed between the characters which have special meanings when used in pairs. That is in: (* (. <> >= <= .) and *).

These Pascal fragments are logically identical:

```
if a = b then begin
    c := hay * (bee - sea) end
```

```
if a=b then begin c:=hay*(bee-sea)end
```

```
if    a   =   b    then    begin
    c    :=    hay    *    ( bee    -    sea
)    end
```

```
if
a
=
b
then
begin
c
:=
hay
*
(
bee
-
sea
)
end
```

## This is different:

```
ifa=bthenbeginc:=hay*(bee-sea)end
```

The first two words are taken to be "ifa" and "bthenbeginc".

# Compilation errors

When a program is compiled, any errors are indicated in a manner something like this:

```
program bad (input, output) ;
var a : integer ;
begin
b := 1 ;
 ↑
 ERROR - UNKNOWN IDENTIFIER

a := a + 1
a := a + 2
↑
 ERROR - SEMICOLON EXPECTED

end.
```

The idea is that the compiler produces another file, called a *listing* file, containing a copy of the program along with messages about any errors. The errors are indicated by an arrow, or other such marker, which points to the place in the program where the compiler detected the error. The marker is followed by an error message or by an error message number. The message numbers have to be looked up in a manual or looked up in a list placed at the end of the listing file. The errors are often confusing, but all they are really saying is that your program does not conform to the syntax diagrams, or breaks one of the other rules given in this chapter.

The first error in the example is clear enough: the variable "b" has not been declared in the variable declaration part. (Identifier is the formal term for names).

The second error in the example is caused by a missing semicolon on the previous line. Notice that the compiler does not detect the absence of the semicolon until it reads the variable name "a", on the following line. Because the marker is actually indicating a correct line in this case, we can see that the way to deal with errors is to study the syntax diagrams carefully and correct the faults accordingly. Avoid adding words or punctuation symbols just because the compiler said they were expected or missing.

Another complication with errors is that an error at the start of a program can cause the compiler to indicate errors in later (correct) parts of the program. An example of this would be if a genuine error in the variable declaration part of a program prevented some variables being declared; there would then be false errors when those variables were used later on in the program. The best advice is to correct the first few errors and try again. Just sticking in whatever the error messages ask for is not sufficient.

As well as producing a listing file, most systems send the error messages to the vdu screen. Since the messages are given out of context, this feature is useless for the purposes of correcting errors unless there are only very few of them. What you need to do is get a printout of the listing file and study it along with the syntax diagrams away from the computer.

## Summary

We can use syntax diagrams to describe languages.

Names in Pascal start with a letter and consist of letters and digits.

The compiler puts a copy of the program with errors marked in a listing file.

# Exercises

Use the syntax diagrams to check if the following Pascal programs are syntactically correct.

```
program one (input, output) ;
var a :integer ;
begin
a := a + 1
end.
```

```
program two(input,output);var a:integer;begin a:=a+1 end.
```

```
program three (input, output) ;
var a : integer ;
begin
a := a + 1
end
end.
```

```
program four (input, output) ;
var a : integer ;
begin
a := a + 1 ;
end.
```

```
program five (input, output) ;
var a, b : integer ;
begin
a := a + 1 ;
b := a + b
end.
```

```
program six (input, output) ;
var a, b : integer ;
begin
a :=
a + 1 ; b :=
a + b
end.
```

# CHAPTER 6
# Calculations with integers

## More on assignment statements

Consider the following assignment statement:

```
age := age + 1
```

It looks a little confusing, especially if we (wrongly) try to think of it as being like an algebraic equation. In a sense it embodies the whole idea of a program as being something that is executed on a computer. It is an instruction to the computer to take the value of the current contents of the variable "age", add one to it and place the result back in the variable, replacing its current contents. In other words, the left hand side refers to a variable that is going to be changed, and the right-hand side specifies the value that will be assigned. If the right hand side refers to the variable that is being changed, the *present* value is taken.

Suppose we have two variables "a" and "b" and we wish to exchange the values they hold; we might try:

```
a := b ;
b := a
```

which will not work. Make sure you understand why not. If necessary, try obeying the sequence using named boxes drawn on paper, before proceeding.

The following code will work correctly because it uses a temporary variable to preserve the value of "a" before changing it.

```
temp := a ;
a := b ;
b := temp
```

# Calculations

The following assignment statements show some examples of the integer (whole number) calculations that are possible in Pascal.

```
x := - ((y + z) * 2) ;
x := y div z ;
```

They are very similar to ordinary algebra with addition and subtraction being represented by "+" and "−". The differences are as follows.

1.  An asterisk (*) is used to indicate multiplication since "x" might be mistaken for a variable.

2.  The multiplication symbol may not be omitted between quantities we want multiply together.

3.  The horizontal line is not available to indicate division, so the dividend and divisor are enclosed in brackets and are placed before and after one of the division operators. A calculation such as:

    $$\frac{a+b}{c-d}$$

    would be written:    $(a + b)$ div $(c − d)$

4.  Since we are dealing with whole numbers, we need to use special forms of divide rather than "/" which is the normal division symbol. The special forms of divide are *div* and *mod*.

*Div* means divide and truncate the answer. Here are some examples to illustrate this:

> 7 div 2 is 3
> 7 div 3 is 2
> −7 div 3 is −2

*Mod* gives the remainder after a division. Here are some examples to illustrate this:

> 7 mod 3 is 1
> 8 mod 3 is 2

It should be obvious that all variables referred to in a calculation must have a value before the computer tries to work out the result of the calculation. Some systems can check, while a program is being executed, whether it attempts to use variables which have not yet been assigned a value. The system would stop executing the program and report what is called a *run-time* error. Such a system would also detect attempts to produce numbers larger than the system can cope with. Division of any number by zero is a good example of such an attempt.

## Brackets

Consider the following assignment statement:

```
a := b + c * d
```

Does it mean: add b and c and multiply the result by d, or does it mean multiply c by d and add the result to b? There are rules, called precedence rules, in Pascal as in algebra which specify what *is* meant by the example. Our advice is forget them and always use brackets where there may be the smallest ambiguity. The above would thus be written as one of these:

```
a := (b + c) * d
a := b + (c * d)
```

## Money, money, money

Calculations involving money are usually done in pennies using integer arithmetic for complete accuracy. Quantities are converted to pounds and pence before being printed.

## Summary

You should now be able to write a program that inputs some numbers, calculates a result from a formula and displays the result.

# Exercises

Design and develop the following programs. During the design, be aware that they do not need selection or repetition as they can both be done using sequences and integer arithmetic.

1.  A program to calculate the total value of a cash payment in decimal coinage. The user should enter seven numbers which represent the number of ones, twos, fives, tens, twenties, fifties and hundreds respectively.

2.  A program that reads in three integers representing the launch time of a balloon expressed in hours, minutes and seconds on the 24-hour clock. It then reads another integer, giving the balloon's flight time in seconds, and calculates the the time of day at which the balloon should return to earth.

# CHAPTER 7
# More on procedures

## Introduction

We have already met the idea of procedures in chapter 4. In this chapter we will first review the idea of a procedure and then we will go on to look at the ideas of local data and parameters.

Procedures are good because they enable us to build large programs from small, manageable pieces. The general structure of a program that uses procedures is like this:

```
program --------- ;

var
      --------
      --------
      -------

procedure -------- ;
begin
---------
---------
-------
end ;

procedure --------- ;
begin
-------
----
------
end ;

begin
------
----
-----
end.
```

We can study a program with this structure in a piecemeal fashion. We can first look at the main program down at the bottom, and get a feel for the overall operation of the program. Then we can look at an individual procedure and similarly find out how it works.

Before we move on, we have to define something that we will refer to several times in this chapter. The part of a procedure declaration from *procedure* to the semicolon is called the *procedure heading*.

## Local variables

Look at the following program that uses a procedure to interchange the values of two numbers:

```
program interchange1 (input, output) ;
var
     a, b, temp : integer ;

procedure swap ;
begin
temp := a ;
a := b ;
b := temp
end ;

begin
read (a, b) ;
swap ;
write (a, b)
end.
```

The variable "temp" is used only within the procedure. In a sense, therefore, it rather clutters up the data at the top of the program. Perhaps it would be better if it could be moved to where it is used - within the procedure. This is exactly what we can do:

```
program interchange2 (input, output) ;
var
     a, b : integer ;

procedure swap ;
var
     temp : integer ;
begin
temp := a ;
a := b ;
b := temp
end ;

begin
read (a, b) ;
swap ;
write (a, b)
end.
```

We have now declared a variable after the procedure heading. Such a variable is called a *local* variable. (The variables at the top of the program are called *global* variables.) Notice that the syntax of the local variable declaration is exactly like that of variables declared at the top of the program.

The general structure of a program that uses local variables is:

```
program ---------- ;

var
        ---------      ←—— global variables
        ---------

procedure -------- ;
var
        ------                ←—— local variables
        -----
begin
---------
---------
-------
end ;

procedure --------- ;
var
        -----                 ←—— local variables
        ------
begin
-------
----
-------
end ;

begin
------
----
-----
end.
```

We now have our data written down in places compatible with its use:

   global data is declared at the top of the program
   and can be referred to throughout the program,

   local data is declared within a particular procedure
   and can only be referred to within that procedure.

The program as a whole is now easier to read and understand because:

the main program is easier to read since it is less cluttered, and

the individual procedures are easier to read because we can more easily see what variables they use.

As a general rule in programming, we should try to minimise the proportion of global data and maximise the proportion of local data.

## Temporary nature of local variables

There is an important difference between local and global variables. Global variables are permanent - they exist all the time that the program is being executed. But, in Pascal, local variables are created when the procedure is entered and destroyed when control leaves the procedure. When a procedure is not being executed, its local variables do not exist. This is demonstrated by the following incorrect program:

```
program interchange3 (input, output) ;
var
     a, b : integer ;

procedure swap ;
var
     temp : integer ;
begin
temp := a ;
a := b ;
b := temp
end ;

begin
read (a, b) ;
write (temp) ;                   { error 1 }
swap ;
write (temp) ;                   { error 2 }
write (a, b)
end.
```

The errors occur because the main program tries to access the procedure's local variable; not only is it not allowed to do so, but the variable has not even been created at the point in the program's execution at which this first occurs, and it has been destroyed by the second time it occurs.

Just as the main program cannot access a procedure's local variables, a procedure cannot access another procedure's local variables.

61

# Name clashes

What happens if we write a program in which there are two or more variables with the same name? This can't happen in a program's global data or within a particular procedure's local data, but it is certainly possible (in Pascal) to have an local variable with the same name as a global variable, or with the same name as another procedure's local variable. For example:

```
program clash (input, output) ;
var
      count : integer ;

procedure first ;
var
      count : integer ;
begin
count := 1
end ;

procedure second ;
var
      count : integer ;
begin
count := count + 1
end ;

begin
count := 3 ;
first ;
second ;
write (count)
end.
```

The answer is that there are two or more different variables with the same name. These variables may exist at the same time. This is a potentially confusing situation and one that should be treated carefully. However, there is a rule for resolving the issue:

within a procedure, the name refers to the *local* variable.

Therefore in the above program the meanings of the references to the variable "count" are as shown by the arrows:

```
        program clash (input, output) ;
        var
              count : integer ;

        procedure first ;
        var
              count : integer ;
        begin
        count := 1
        end ;

        procedure second ;
        var
              count : integer ;
        begin
        count := count + 1
        end ;

        begin
        count := 3 ;
        first ;
        second ;
        write (count)
        end.
```

In the "clash" program, therefore, the value of the global "count" will still be three when it is printed, because both procedures only effect their local "count"s.

## The use of local variables during design

There is no need to consider local variables during the design of an algorithm. All variable declarations should be introduced as the pseudo-code is converted to Pascal. Any variables which are needed while the main algorithm is being converted must be declared in the main program, and will therefore be global variables. Any variables which are needed while a mini-algorithm is being converted should be declared after the procedure's heading and will be local to that procedure.

## Parameters

Let us have another look at the program to interchange the value of two numbers. Suppose that we wanted to extend it to change the order of four numbers. Suppose that the program is to print the numbers starting with the second one and followed by the first, fourth and third numbers. The program might be as follows:

```
program interchange4 (input, output) ;
var
      a, b, c, d : integer ;

procedure swapAB ;
var
      temp : integer ;
begin
temp := a ;
a := b ;
b := temp
end ;

procedure swapCD ;
var
      temp : integer ;
begin
temp := c ;
c := d ;
d := temp
end ;

begin
read (a, b, c, d) ;
swapAB ;
swapCD ;
write (a, b, c, d)
end.
```

Common sense should tell us that it must be unnecessary to have two almost identical versions of the swap procedure. The purpose of using computers should be to free people from boring repetitive tasks, therefore, we should look for a better solution whenever we are tempted to write anything like the above.

Another, equally important, problem with the program is that the sending of information to the procedure (and the return of information from it) is done using global variables. There are several snags with this. To use the swap procedures, we have to:

> know the names of the variables that they use,

> use these names even if they are inconvenient, and

> search around in the global data to see what is going on.

A possible solution to the duplicated-procedure problem might be to have one procedure and to introduce a couple of global variables for the procedure to work on. Then we could move the numbers to be swapped into those global variables before calling the swap procedure, and get them back afterwards. This would, however, make the second set of problems even worse!

The use of parameters solves all these problems. Here is how we can call the procedure swap using parameters:

```
-

-

read (a, b, c, d) ;
swap (a, b) ;
swap (c, d) ;
write (a, b, c, d)
```

The data items that we wish the procedure to work on are written in brackets after the procedure name. They are called the *actual parameters*. They describe what data items from the outside world the procedure will operate on. In the above program fragment, we can see that:

the first time the procedure "swap" is called, it is to work on "a" and "b", and

the second time it is to work on "c" and "d".

The procedure is now written like this:

```
procedure swap (var n1, n2 :integer) ;
var
        temp : integer ;
begin
temp := n1 ;
n1 := n2 ;
n2 := temp
end ;
```

The parameters that appear in the procedure heading are called *formal parameters*. Pascal behaves as if the formal parameter names ("n1" and "n2" in our example) were *aliases* for whichever variables are in the list of actual parameters at any of the of procedure's calls. This means that the first time "swap" is called, the main program's variable "a" is actually used, instead of "n1", whenever the procedure refers to "n1". Similarly, the main program's variable "b" is actually used whenever the procedure refers to "n2". The second time "swap" is called, the main program's variable "c" is used whenever the procedure text refers to "n1", and the main program's variable "d" is used whenever the procedure text refers to "n2".

Formal parameters are so called because they determine the *form* the actual parameters must take whenever the procedure is called. By form we mean the *number* of parameters and the *type* of the parameters. We see, therefore, that "swap" *must* be given two integer variables to work on. The following procedure call would not be allowed:

```
swap (a, b, c)
```

because there are three actual parameters, not two as specified in the procedure's declaration.

The following would also not be allowed:

```
swap (a, e)
```

if either variable was not an integer.

It is the *order* of the items in a list of actual parameters which decides which one is to be used for each formal parameter. The rule is that the first actual parameter corresponds to the first formal parameter, the second actual parameter corresponds to the second formal parameter, and so on.

Notice that formal parameters are only declared in the procedure heading. There would be a compilation error if a local variable was declared with the same name as one of the formal parameters.

Notice also, that the names of the actual and formal parameters need not be the same (though they could be).

The use of parameters enhances a program for a number of reasons. First, we avoid duplicating procedures. Second, we can clearly see what data items a procedure works upon. Third, we are avoiding the use of global data for communication with procedures. Finally, we do not need to know what names a procedure uses to refer to the data that it acts upon.

# An artificial example

The interchange program is a rather artificial example. Because it is short and simple, it is a good program to illustrate the use of local variables and parameters; but did you notice that changing the order of the items could be done more easily by:

```
read   (a, b, c, d) ;
write  (b, a, d, c)
```

# The use of parameters during design

What we have done so far in considering parameters has been rather odd - we took a program and changed it, without changing the pseudo-code. Normally we would introduce parameters during the design of an algorithm.

Let's examine designing and writing a procedure from scratch. For example, suppose we need to write a program to print the square and cube of the numbers from one to 20. The algorithm will probably contain some pseudo-code like this:

```
for number = 1 to 20 do
        print number
        power := 2
        raise to power
        print square
        power := 3
        raise to power
        print cube
        start new line
endfor
```

Note that one general procedure, "raise to power", has been used rather than one procedure to square a number and another, similar but separate one, to cube a number.

We can now clarify the design by writing the names of the things that "raise to power" will use or change. We will write the quantities in brackets after each procedure call. If we do that the design is:

```
for number = 1 to 20 do
     print number
     power := 2
     raise to power (number, power, square)
     print square
     power := 3
     raise to power (number, power, cube)
     print cube
     start new line
endfor
```

When the algorithm is converted to Pascal, "number", "power", "square" and "cube" will all be variables belonging to the main program. They must be passed to the procedure as actual parameters. The program will read better if we call the procedure "raise" so that the procedure calls look like this:

```
raise (number, power, square);
raise (number, power, cube);
```

When we design the procedure, we should bear in mind that it will have three parameters - a number, a power to which the number is to be raised and a variable which is to receive the result of the calculation. As we have seen, we don't need to stick to the main algorithm's names for the parameters. In fact we need neither know nor care what names the main algorithm uses for the variables it passes to the procedure. All that we need to ensure is that we have the correct number of parameters, and that they are in the same order as when the main algorithm passed them. In our example the best, most general names, for the formal parameters are number, power and result. Therefore the algorithm we have to write for "raise" is simply one to calculate the result when a number if raised to a power.

The pseudo code for the procedure is :

```
raise (number, power, result)

result := 1
for count := 1 to power do
     result := result * number
endfor
```

When we convert the pseudo-code to Pascal, the procedure heading will be:

```
procedure raise (var number, power, answer : integer) ;
```

Notice that we have specified the type of variables the procedure will operate upon.

# Modular programs

A modular program is one that is constructed from small units (procedures) that are as independent of each other as possible. Modular programs are easier to understand and maintain. The use of local variables and parameters makes procedures independent and self-contained and leads to more modular programs.

In a modular program, we could:

> make major changes to the internal working of any procedure, without having even having to consider the rest of the program;

> completely remove a procedure, without having to worry about leaving its variables cluttering up the main program wasting the time of all the future readers of the program; or

> move a procedure to another program, without having to find out what data we need to take with it, and without needing to change the procedure to use the variable names that the new program uses for the data the procedure works on.

If all the data is global and parameters are not used, there is no easy way of knowing which procedures change or refer to particular data items, the program would not be modular and the above changes would not be so easy.

# Formal parameter names

When we write a new program we often want to use procedures that have already been written (as part of some other program). It is therefore a good idea for formal parameter names to be as general as possible. This was the case with the "swap" procedure earlier in the chapter. The names "n1" and "n2" are perfectly suitable for use on any occasion that two numbers have to be swapped. This would not be the case if we had called them anything to do with the names of the variables in the program from which the procedure was taken. Those variable names should have been chosen specifically for that program and would probably not be the most suitable for the new program.

# A puzzle

Here is a program which uses parameters and local variables. What do you think
the program prints?

```
program puzzle (input, output) ;
var
     x, y, z : integer ;

procedure a (var p, q : integer) ;
var
     x : integer ;
begin
x := p * p ;
                                                    ←——————————————————— Point 5
q := p + x
                                                    ←——————————————————— Point 2
end ;

procedure b (var z : integer) ;
begin
                                                    ←——————————————————— Point 4
a (z, z)
end ;

begin
x := 1 ;
z := 2 ;
                                                    ←——————————————————— Point 1
a (x, y) ;
                                                    ←——————————————————— Point 3
b (z) ;
                                                    ←——————————————————— Point 6
write (x, y, z)
end.
```

To check that the program does what we think it does, we will go through it and
mimic its actions on paper.

70

At the point labelled 1 in the program, the state of the variables is as follows:

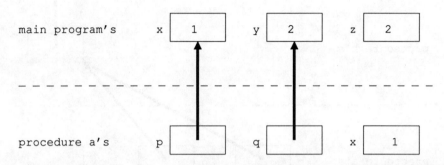

At point 2 in the program, the state is:

Remember that, in procedure "a", "p" and "q" are aliases for the actual parameters that were passed to the procedure when it was called. Therefore "p" really means the main program's variable "x" which was the first actual parameter when the procedure was called, and "q" really means the main program's variable "y" which was the second parameter.

At point 3 in the program, the state is:

main program's     x    1     y    2     z    2

because "a"'s parameters and variables have been destroyed.

At point 4 in the program, the state is:

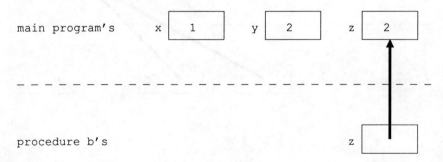

At point 5 in the program, the state is:

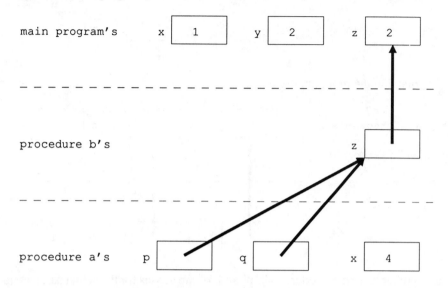

At point 2 (again) in the program, the state is:

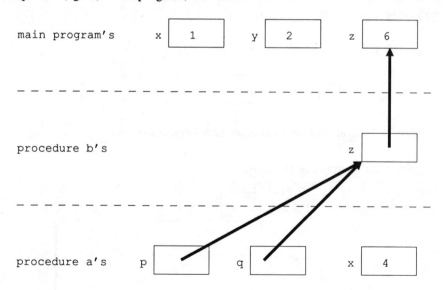

At point 6 in the program, the state is:

`main program's`   x $\boxed{1}$   y $\boxed{2}$   z $\boxed{6}$

and these are the values displayed.

The exercise is difficult because of the abstract nature of the program and because of the meaningless variable names, but it does serve to illustrate the operation of parameters and local variables.

## Revised syntax diagrams

These diagrams cover the syntax of parameters and local variables:

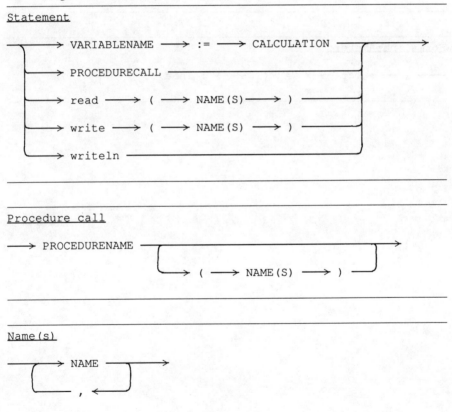

Statement

Procedure call

Name(s)

## Procedure declaration

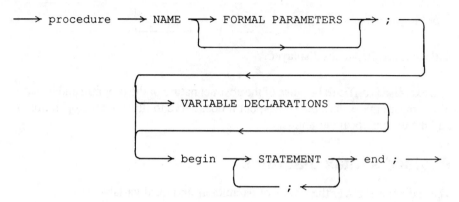

## Formal parameters

$\longrightarrow$ ( $\longrightarrow$ var $\longrightarrow$ NAME(S) $\longrightarrow$ : integer ) $\longrightarrow$

# Summary

Procedures are essential in making programs easier to design and understand. They allow us to build programs from manageable pieces.

Local data is data that is declared and used only within a particular procedure. It cannot be used by any other procedure. Local data therefore highlights what data a procedure is using to do its job. The use of local data reduces the size of global data and thereby improves the readability and modularity of a program.

Using parameters reduces the need for sets of nearly identical procedures. The use of parameters also ensures that the data that is passed to and from a procedure is explicitly described, rather than being lumped in with all the other global data. It also makes it possible to use a procedure without having to know the names that the procedure uses to refer to the data that it works on.

In summary, procedures are an excellent way of imparting structure to a program - but local data and parameters make procedures even better.

Global data should be eliminated or reduced as much as possible.

# Exercises

1. Write a procedure to display the message:

   Hello welcome

   on the terminal screen. Show how someone would use the procedure.

2. Write a procedure that calculates how much change a shop assistant should give the customer. Decide what parameters are necessary and show how the procedure would be used.

3. Look at the programs that you have already written and see how they could be improved by using local data.

4. Look at the algorithms and programs that you have already written and see how they could be improved by using parameters.

# CHAPTER 8

# Repetition and selection in Pascal

## Repetition

We have already seen the use of the *while* statement to carry out repetition in pseudo-code. Here is an example of a Pascal program using a *while* statement to display the integers 0 to 999:

```
program display (input, output) ;
var
     number : integer ;
begin
number := 0 ;
while number <= 999 do begin
     write (number) ;
     writeln ;
     number := number + 1 end ;
writeln
end.
```

Note the similarity of the Pascal to pseudo-code. The rules for translating pseudo-code's *while* statement into Pascal are:

1.  place the word *begin* after the word *do*,

2.  remove the word *endwhile*,

3.  add the word *end* at the end of the line before the removed *endwhile*,

4.  insert the semicolons.

It is important to note that we have to add an *end* for every removed *endwhile* even if one or more *ends* have already been added while converting other pseudo-code to Pascal.

The rules for putting in semicolons are as before, and the above program fragment illustrates them. Semi-colons separate statements one from another. Put another way, we place a semicolon after every statement, but not before the word *end*.

Notice that there is no semicolon after the word *begin*. Also note that in the example there is a semicolon after *end* to separate the whole *while* statement from the *writeln* which follows it.

Remember that the condition checking is done at the start, and the body of the loop is done if the condition is true. Otherwise the statement following the *while* is done. If the condition is false the first time, the body *never* gets done.

The syntax chart for the *while* statement is:

while statement

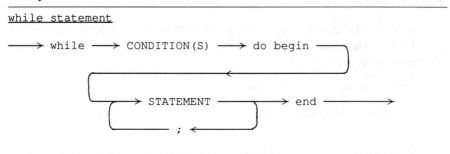

The comparisons that can appear in conditions are given in this table:

| Operator (in English) | Pascal equivalent |
|---|---|
| greater than | > |
| less than | < |
| equal to | = |
| greater than or equal to | >= |
| less than or equal to | <= |
| not equal to | <> |

Here is another example. The problem is to read and display numbers until a number greater than 6000 is encountered.

```
program echo (input, output) ;
var
      number : integer ;
begin
while number <= 6000 do begin
      read (number) ;
      write (number) ;
      writeln end
end.
```

Unfortunately, this program is wrong! Can you see why?

The problem with the program is that the first time the value of the variable "number" is tested (in the *while* statement), it does not have a properly defined value. No previous statement has given it a value. We leave it as an exercise for the reader to fix the problem.

Let us look at another program. The program is to input a set of numbers, ending with a negative number, calculate their sum, and count how many numbers there are. First we design the program, using pseudo-code:

```
set up counters
read first number
while more numbers do
      add to counters
      read number
endwhile
display answers
```

Then we take the pseudo-code and translate it into Pascal:

```
program calculate (input, output) ;
var
      sum, count, number : integer ;
begin
sum := 0 ;
count := 0 ;
read (number) ;
while number >= 0 do begin
      sum := sum + number ;
      count := count + 1 ;
      read (number) end ;
write (sum, count)
end.
```

# Repetition using for

As in pseudo-code, if we want to do something a known number of times we can usually use the *for* statement. In certain circumstances it may show what we are wanting to do more clearly than using a *while* statement. Here is an example of a program to calculate the squares of the integers from one to ten.

```
program squares (input, output) ;
var
      square, number : integer ;
begin
for number := 1 to 10 do begin
      square := number * number ;
      write (square) ;
      writeln end
end.
```

Notice that, in this example, the value of the variable "number" is used in the body of the loop.

The rules for translating pseudo-code's *for* statement into Pascal are:

1. place the word *begin* after the word *do*,

2. remove the word *endfor*,

3. add the word *end* at the end of the line before the removed *endfor*,

4. insert the semicolons.

The syntax chart for a *for* statement is:

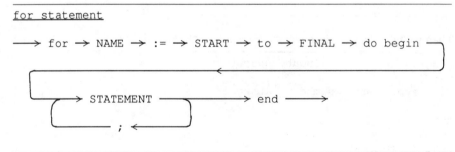

for statement

The body of the loop is first executed with the value of the integer variable, NAME, set to the starting value. Thereafter the body is repeated with the integer variable incremented in steps of one. Finally, the loop is executed with the variable set to the final value. If the starting value and final value are equal, the body is obeyed just once. The starting and final values can be either integer numbers or integer variables.

Here is a program in which the variable referred to in the *for* statement is not used in the body of the loop. The program calculates 100 pseudo-random numbers in various ranges.

```
program random (input, output) ;
var
      random, random0Or1, random1To6,
      randomDigit, count : integer ;
begin
random := 12345 ;
for count := 1 to 100 do begin
      random0Or1 := random div (65536 div 2) ;
      random1To6 := (random mod 6) + 1 ;
      randomDigit := random mod 10 ;
      write (random, random0Or1, random1To6, randomDigit) ;
      writeln ;
      random := ((random * 25173) + 13849) mod 65536 end
end.
```

See how the pseudo-random numbers are generated. The first assignment statement sets up what is known as the *seed* or starting value of "random". The first three statements inside the loop use "random" in calculating the random numbers in the different ranges. The last statement in the loop sets up a new value of "random" for future use. The program always generates the same sequences of numbers. It could be improved by making it ask the user to supply the seed value. Find out whether your system has its own method of generating random numbers. If you use it, remember that it will not be standard Pascal (unlike the above program) and it will not be possible to transfer the program to another computer without having to modify it.

The magic numbers in the above program may cause problems on some very small computers. In that case use 123, 69, 173 and 256 instead of 12345, 25173, 13849 and 65536 respectively.

# Selection in Pascal

Again selection in Pascal is similar to pseudo-code, but with *begin* and *end* and no *endif*. Here is an example:

```
if balance < 0 then begin
     write ('no credit') end
else begin
     balance := balance - debit end
```

The rules for translating pseudo-code's *if - then - else* statement into Pascal are:

1.  place the word *begin* after the words *then* and *else*,

2.  remove the word *endif*,

3.  add the word *end* at the end of the last line before the *else* and the end of the last line before the removed *endif*,

4.  insert the semicolons.

The syntax chart for *if* statements is:

if statement

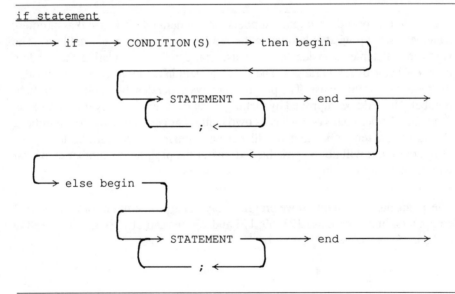

# More complex conditions

In some problems it is necessary to be able to specify more complex tests. For example:

```
if (age > 18) and (age < 65) then begin
    payTaxes end
```

The word "and" is a Pascal word that allows two (or more) conditions to be tested within a single *if* or *while* statement. Note that the individual conditions are within brackets. This is not only desirable for clarity, but is actually needed in Pascal. In addition to the *and* operator, we can use *or* and *not*, as in:

```
if (a > b) or (c < d) and not (e = f) then begin
    something end
```

Note that
    not (x = y)
has exactly the same meaning as:
    x <> y

As in mathematics, there are rules in Pascal that specify how the result of a complex condition like the above is to be worked out. As before, we advise that the clearest thing is to use brackets if there is any possible ambiguity. The previous *if* statement should therefore be written like this:

```
if ((a > b) or (c < d)) and (not (e = f)) then begin
    something end
```

or possibly, depending on what we require, like this:

```
if (a > b) or ((c < d) and (not (e = f))) then begin
    something end
```

But we should be warned: if we find ourselves using conditions that are as complicated as these examples, we should suspect that there is an easier way to describe what we want to do.

# Summary

Selection and repetition in Pascal are very similar to selection and repetition in pseudo-code. There are simple rules for converting a pseudo-code design into Pascal.

# Exercises - repetition

1. Convert to a *for* loop:

```
y := 18 ;
while y < 43 do begin
        y := y + 1 ;
        write (y) ;
        writeln end
```

2. Convert to a *while* loop

```
for count := n to m do begin
        write (count) end
```

3. Use the syntax diagrams to check the syntax of these *while* statements. Correct them, assuming that the indentation correctly shows the programmer's intention.

```
while a < b do
        a := a + 1 ;
writeln
```

```
while a < b do begin
        a := a + 1 end ;
writeln
```

```
while a < b do begin
        a := a + 1 ;
        x := x + a end
writeln
```

```
while a < b do begin
        a := a + 1 ;
        x := x + a ; end ;
writeln
```

Develop programs to do the following:

4. Calculate the compound interest on £100 invested at 12% for six years. Discard fractions less than 50/100 of a penny and round other fractions up to the next penny when calculating the annual interest. Don't forget to use integer arithmetic.

5. A piece of paper is 1mm thick. Calculate how thick it will be if folded 8 times.

6. How many terms of the series $1 + 2 + 3 + 4$ .... are needed so that the sum is greater than 10000?

7.  Display a box like this on the vdu screen:

    ```
    ****
    *  *
    *  *
    *  *
    ****
    ```

8.  Same as above, but this time the user of the program can key in the size (height and width) of the box.

9.  Calculate the factorial of a number that is keyed in as data. The factorial of 5 is 5 x 4 x 3 x 2 x 1 = 120.

## Exercises - selection

Develop programs to do the following:

1.  Input three numbers and sort them into ascending numerical order.

2.  Play a game called "which hand". The computer randomly selects a hand (left or right) and asks the player to guess which one the sweet is in. The player enters -1, for left, or 1, for right. The computer responds with an appropriate message.

## Exercises - general

Develop programs to do the following:

1.  Find the largest, smallest and sum of 10 numbers keyed in as data.

2.  As above, but there can be any number of numbers, ending with a value of -10,000.

3.  As above, but the first number entered is the number of following numbers which make up the data.

4.  Play the game of "Nim". The computer creates three piles of matches, each with a random number of matches in it. It then chooses (randomly) who starts - you or the computer. Each of the two players (you and the computer) goes alternately. You can remove as many matches as you like from any one pile. You must remove at least one. The winner is the person who forces his or her opponent to take the last match. The computer should play by choosing a pile and a quantity at random. You specify what you want to do by giving a pile number and a number of matches.

# CHAPTER 9
# Processing character data

So far we have seen only seen one type of variable - integer. Variables may also be declared to hold characters so that programs can deal with alphabetic data, such as names and addresses. We declare character variables just like integer variables, but we use the word *char* to specify the variable's type. For example:

```
var   a, b : char ;
      x, y : integer ;
```

In main memory, we might visualize the effect of the above as:

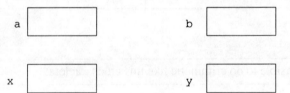

Note that an individual character variable (a box in main memory) can hold just one character. This means that if, for example, we want to manipulate someone's name, we will need several character variables.

## Reading character data

A *read* into a *char* variable does *not* skip over blanks (spaces) - as is the case when reading an integer. The next character keyed in (whatever it is) is placed in the variable. For example if we declare:

```
var  ch1, ch2, ch3, ch4 : char ;
```

and carry out the actions:

```
read (ch1, ch2, ch3, ch4) ;
write (ch2, ch3, ch4, ch1) ;
```

What happens with each of the following lines of data?

```
1234
1 234
a*7 b
'b'a                    Note the position of the spaces.
```

The outputs would be:

```
2341
 231
*7 a
b'a'
```

If we want to give a character variable a value by means of an assignment, we write the character in quotes:

```
ch1 := 'a' ;
ch2 := '*' ;
ch3 := '7'
```

It is *not* possible or sensible to do arithmetic like this on characters:

```
ch1 := ch2 + '3'
```

## Readln

Sometimes we want our program to skip anything that remains on the current line and go on to the start of the next line. *Readln* does this. For example, suppose we entered this data:

```
*anything at all
!something else
```

The effect of this:

```
read (ch1) ;
readln ;
read (ch2) ;
write (ch1, ch2)
```

would be to print:

```
*!
```

Here is another program which uses character variables.

```
program swap (input, output) ;
var
     count, max, number : integer ;
     ch1, ch2, ch3, ch4, ch5 : char ;
begin
read (max) ;
readln ;
for count := 1 to max do begin
     read (ch1, ch2, ch3, ch4) ;
     read (number) ;
     read (ch5) ;
     readln ;
     write (ch5) ;
     write (number) ;
     write (ch1, ch2, ch3, ch4) ;
     writeln end
end.
```

What does it do if it is given the following inputs?

```
3
ball1x
bats    235y
feet4z
```

Answer - it prints this:

```
x       1ball
y       235bats
z       4feet
```

Notice that, when made to read an integer variable, Pascal ignores the leading spaces (if any) and leaves the first character after the integer unread, so that it would be the first character involved in the next read.

Here is the specification of a problem for which we want to write a program. We need to maintain a count of the number of boxes of cornflakes in stock.

When boxes are received, we key:

    r   followed by the amount

When boxes are issued, we key:

    i   followed by the amount

When we have finished, we key:

    q

Here is a program to maintain the count:

```
program cornflakes (input, output) ;
var
      command : char ;
      quantity, total : integer ;
begin
total := 0 ;
read (command) ;
while command <> 'q' do begin
      read (quantity) ;
      if command = 'i' then begin
          total := total - quantity end
      else begin
          total := total + quantity end ;
      readln ;
      read (command) end ;
write ('You have ', total, ' boxes')
end.
```

Note that the program does no checking; any command which is not "i" or "q" is taken to be "r".

Here is another example. It is often necessary in text processing programs to skip the spaces at the start of a line. Here is a procedure to do that:

```
procedure getFirstNonBlank (var character : char) ;
begin
read (character) ;
while character = ' ' do begin
      read (character) end
end ;
```

Notice that the procedure passes the first non-blank character back to the calling procedure using the formal parameter "character".

## Testing for the end of line

Sometimes, in a program, we need to know when the end of a line of text has been reached. For example, suppose we wanted to count the characters on a line, we could use the following procedure:

```
procedure measureLine (var length : integer) ;
var
     character : char ;
begin
length := 0 ;
while not eoln do begin
     read (character) ;
     length := length + 1 end
end
```

This procedure is testing the value of something called "eoln" (short for "end of line"). It is a bit like a variable whose value is changed, by the system, to reflect the status of the input. Will the procedure work correctly if there are no characters on the line?

## Comparison of characters

It should be clear that this program:

```
program compare1 (input, output) ;
var
     a, b : integer ;
begin
a := 1 ;
b := 2 ;
if a > b then begin
     write ('a greater than b') end
else begin
     write ('b greater than a') end
end.
```

will print "b greater than a". What does this version, which uses characters rather than integers, do?

```
program compare2 (input, output) ;
var
     a, b : char ;
begin
a := 'c' ;
b := 'd' ;
if a > b then begin
     write ('a greater than b') end
else begin
     write ('b greater than a') end
end.
```

It does, in fact, print the same message. This is because with character variables, ">" is taken to mean "comes after in the alphabet", instead of "is greater than". Similarly, "<" is taken to mean "comes before in the alphabet", instead of "is less than". The following relationships apply on all computer systems:

$$'a' < 'b' < 'c' .. 'y' < 'z'$$
$$'A' < 'B' < 'C' .. 'Y' < 'Z'$$
$$'0' < '1' < '2' .. '8' < '9'$$

Whether the following are true or not varies from system to system:

$$'a' < 'A'$$
$$'a' < '9'$$
$$'A' < '9'$$

The relationship of the space character and the punctuation characters to each other and to the letters and digits also varies between different computer systems.

The ability to compare characters in this way is very important: it allows us to write programs which put things into alphabetical order.

## Character variables as parameters

If we needed to write a procedure which operated on two integers and two letters, the procedure heading might look like this:

```
procedure something (var c1 : char ; var n1 : integer ;
                     var c2 : char ; var n2 : integer) ;
```

Notice that it is quite alright for the procedure heading to take up more than one line.

Notice, also, that the word *var* occurs four times in the procedure heading. If we used this procedure heading:

```
procedure something (var c1, c2 : char ; var n1, n2 :
integer) ;
```

and changed the order of the actual parameters throughout the program, we would still have had to repeat the word *var*. We have to use *var* whenever a formal parameter follows a formal parameter of a different type.

## Revised syntax diagrams

These diagrams cover the syntax of character variables and parameters:

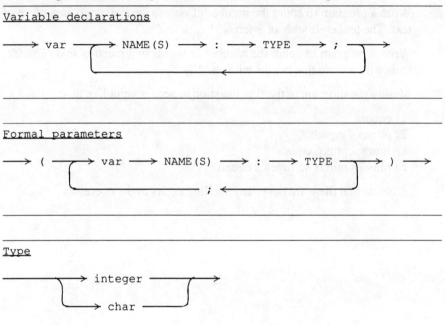

Variable declarations

Formal parameters

Type

## Summary

Variables of type *char* allow text (letters, spaces, punctuation symbols) to be processed. We can input characters, output them and compare them. We do this one character at a time.

## Exercises

1.  Write a pocket calculator program capable of evaluating things like:

    11=
    22–7=
    17*4+6=
    23+78–45*2=

    Assume the operators will be evaluated left to right, and that there will no brackets.

2.  Write a program to count the number of non-space characters in a piece of text. The text ends with an asterisk (*).

3.  Write a program to count the number of words in a piece of text. The text ends with a word that begins with an '*'.

4.  Modify the program in the first question to accept input like this:

    11 equals
    22 minus 7 equals
    17 times 4 plus 6 equals
    23 plus 78 minus 45 times 2 equals

    Assume that there are never any spelling errors in the operators.

# CHAPTER 10
# A case study in design and coding

In this chapter we describe the development of a complete program from design to coding. Here is the program specification.

A person plays games of "which hand" with the computer, using an interactive terminal. The computer chooses a hand, left or right, randomly. The user guesses the hand and keys in "l" or "r". The computer tells the user whether they guessed correctly. It then asks whether the user wants to continue. If they don't, it displays the score and stops.

It is most important that we carefully examine the specification, making sure that we understand it completely and that there are no ambiguities or omissions. If we do identify any lack of clarity, we should go back to the person who wrote the specification, sort out the problem, and then revise the specification.

One way to start would be to write something like:

```
wins := wins + 1
losses := losses + 1
etc
```

But this would be no good at all ! This would be starting with some of the detail of the program - like starting to design a new car by thinking about how big the steering wheel is to be. In contrast, the recommended approach is to design the overall structure first and the detail later. Certainly, we should not even think about the programming language code until the design is complete.

Here then is an attempt at the overall algorithm:

```
while more games do
     play a game (wins, losses)
     decide what next (more games)
endwhile
display totals (wins, losses)
```

Next we might refine (as a procedure):

```
play a game (wins, losses)

     choose (hand)
     invite (guess)
     compare (hand, guess)
     display appropriate message (hand, guess)
     update totals (wins, losses, hand, guess)
```

And now:

```
choose (hand)

     random0Or1 := random div (65536 div 2)
     get next (random)
     if random0Or1 = 0 then
          hand := 'l'
     else
          hand := 'r'
     endif
```

At this stage we have a problem. "Random" must always hold the next available random value. If a local variable were used for "random" when the design was translated to Pascal, the latest value would be lost at the end of the "choose" procedure. (Remember that local variables only exist while a procedure is being executed). Therefore we must make "random" one of the main program's variables, and pass it as a parameter to any procedures which need it.

Amending the design to allow for that gives the following:

```
get seed (random)
while more games do
     play a game (random, wins, losses)
     decide what next (more games)
endwhile
display totals (wins, losses)
```

<u>play a game (random, wins, losses)</u>

```
     choose (random, hand)
     invite (guess)
     compare (hand, guess)
     display appropriate message (hand, guess)
     update totals (wins, losses, hand, guess)
```

<u>choose (random, hand)</u>

```
     random00r1 := random div (65536 div 2)
     get next (random)
     if random00r1 = 0 then
         hand := 'l'
     else
         hand := 'r'
     endif
```

Continuing to refine more of the design we get:

<u>invite (guess)</u>

```
     display prompt
     get guess
     while guess not 'l' or 'r' do
         display error message
         get guess
     endwhile
```

Note that the algorithm checks its inputs. If values other than the expected ones were accepted, the program would not work correctly. It is good practice ,therefore, to guard against incorrect inputs.

If we now look at "compare", we find that we want to use an if statement, but we have nothing to do:

compare (hand, guess)

```
    if guess = hand then
        ?????
```

The conclusion is that this step is part of "display appropriate message". We should therefore delete it from "play a game".

We go on refining components:

display appropriate message (guess, hand)

```
    if guess = hand then
        display right message
    else
        display wrong message
    endif
```

update totals (wins, losses, hand, guess)

```
    if guess = hand then
        wins := wins +1
    else
        losses := losses + 1
    endif
```

decide what next (reply)

```
    display prompt
    get reply
    while reply not 'y' or 'n' do
        display error message
        get reply
    endwhile
```

display totals (wins, losses)

```
    write wins
    write losses
    goodbye
```

The design is now complete. Next we should check it. Is anything missing? Can we do anything in a different way? If we can find another way, which is better? We read the program in the way that it written - from the top.

Now we code the program from the design. We find that as we do so, we need to create variables. The first one is probably the integer variable "random" discussed above. We might well choose to code the program in the same order that we designed it, starting with the main program. Here is the complete program:

```
program whichHand (input, output) ;
var
     random, wins, losses : integer ;
     moreGames            : char ;

procedure getNext (var random : integer) ;
begin
random := ((random * 25173) + 13849) mod 65536
end ;

procedure choose (var random : integer ; var hand : char) ;
var
     random0Or1 : integer ;
begin
random0Or1 := random div (65536 div 3) ;
getNext (random) ;
if random0Or1 = 0 then begin
     hand := 'l' end
else begin
     hand := 'r' end
end ;

procedure invite (var guess : char) ;
begin
write ('Choose a hand (l or r)') ;
writeln ;
read (guess) ;
readln ;
while (guess <> 'l') and (guess <> 'r') do begin
     write ('Please answer l or r') ;
     writeln ;
     read (guess) ;
     readln end
end ;
```

```
procedure displayAppropriateMessage (var guess, hand : char) ;
begin
if guess = hand then begin
     write ('Correct') end
else begin
     write ('Wrong') end ;
writeln
end ;


procedure updateTotals (var wins, losses : integer ;
                        var hand, guess : char) ;
begin
if guess = hand then begin
     wins := wins + 1 end
else begin
     losses := losses + 1 end
end ;


procedure playAGame (var random, wins, losses : integer) ;
var
     hand, guess : char ;
begin
choose (random, hand) ;
invite (guess) ;
displayAppropriateMessage (guess, hand) ;
updateTotals (wins, losses, hand, guess)
end ;


procedure decideWhatNext (var reply : char) ;
begin
write ('Do you wish to play again?') ;
writeln ;
read (reply) ;
while (reply <> 'y') and (reply <> 'n') do begin
     write ('Please answer y or n') ;
     writeln ;
     read (reply) ;
     readln end
end ;
```

```
procedure displayTotals (var wins, losses : integer) ;
begin
write ('You won ', wins, ' game(s) and lost ') ;
write (losses, ' game(s)') ;
writeln ;
write ('Goodbye  - thankyou for playing') ;
writeln
end ;

procedure getSeed (var random : integer) ;
begin
random := 12345
end ;

begin
getSeed (random) ;
moreGames := 'y' ;
while moreGames = 'y' do begin
     playAGame (random, wins, losses) ;
     decideWhatNext (moreGames) end ;
displayTotals (wins, losses)
end.
```

Finally we check the code. Does it match up with the design? Are all the variables that are used declared? Are semicolons in the right places? Have we left out any *begin* or *end* words?

Although we have been systematic and careful, this program has some errors in it. This is the usual situation; it is nearly impossible to design and code a program that is correct. Finding and fixing errors is something we look at later.

## Summary

This program is fairly small, but not trivial. It exhibits the value of first designing the program using pseudo-code and then coding it.

# CHAPTER 11
# Program layout

In using Pascal, there is great scope to lay out a program in a great variety of ways. But a programmer always has to remember that in all probability several other programmers will have to read his or her program during its lifetime in order to correct or amend it. So the aim should always be to write programs in such a way that it is easy for other people to read them. In this chapter we will discuss:

> choosing names for procedures and data
> using indentation
> using blank lines
> using new pages
> using comments.

By looking at alternatives, we will try to arrive at good rules for writing clear comprehensible programs.

## Names

This program is very amusing:

```
program mary (input, output) ;
var
     had, a, little : integer ;
     lamb : char ;

procedure itsFleece ;
  etc
```

but it is rather meaningless (as a program).

What about:

```
program x (input, output) ;
var
     p, q, r : integer ;
     addr : char ;

procedure cwgs ;
  etc
```

Here the names are all rather cryptic - rather like variables in mathematics. Does "cwgs" mean calculate wages, or country and western goes swell?

How about these as guidelines:

"Use long names".

"Avoid short names".

These are no good: a long name is not necessarily more descriptive than a small one. (Why say "small furry mouse-catching mammal" when we mean cat?) So finally we arrive at the following rule:

Use names that describe what you are using them for.

We are referring here to both data and procedure names (but unfortunately we are usually limited to some maximum number of characters).

Procedure names should tell the whole story. If a procedure calculates something and prints it, it would be very misleading to just call it "calculate", rather than "calculateAndPrint". However, such a procedure should probably have been two distinct procedures anyway. It is better to split tasks in a logical way between procedures, so that each procedure does just one thing.

In most Pascal systems, names can consist of both upper and lower case letters. One way of exploiting this is to use lower case normally, except where we have a name that consists of more than one word. In such a case we can start new words (within the name) with upper-case letters. We do this throughout this book.

Text editors usually provide a means of changing every occurrence of a word in a program. So if we think of a better, clearer name for a procedure or variable during the development of a program, we should make the change - it will be a small effort for us, but a big help to the reader.

# Indentation

Indentation is the use of spaces to convey visually the structure of a program. For example:

```
-------
-------
-------
if ------- then begin
    -------
    ------- end
else begin
    ------
    ------ end ;
-------
-------
```

The indentation gives us considerable visual help in seeing the decision structure. We can do the same with *while* and *for* statements.

Some computer systems have a program that will take a untidy Pascal program and convert it into a nicely indented version. Such a program is called a prettyprinter; it can save the programmer a lot of time.

# New pages

Many computer systems provide a facility to tell the system where to start a new page on a listing of a program. Sometimes this is is done by inserting a special command at the appropriate place in the program. New pages can add considerably to the readability of a program. At one extreme we could place just one procedure by itself on a page. Another possibility is to group procedures that are related in some way. For example, they might all act upon the same data item, or they all might contribute towards the same task. What is absolutely awful to read, however, is code that spills over from one page to another - especially when the new page comes right in the middle of the indented coding in the middle of an *if* or *while* statement.

# Comments

Comments are explanations of a piece of program, written in English, and specially distinguished from statements in the programming language. In Pascal we write comments by putting them between curly brackets (braces). Unfortunately, some terminals and printers don't have these characters. If we have to use such a system, we can use ( * to start a comment and * ) to end one. Comments can go *anywhere*, except within a name or a special word. For example:

```
program chess (input, output) ;
{ this program plays -------
----------------------------
---------------------------- }

var    etc
```

Where is it best to use comments? How about the following guideline?

"Use comments when you have some complicated code to explain".

For example:

```
{ swap new and old.    WARNING:    This only works if one
variable has a value of 1 and the other has a value of 2 }
old := new ;
new := 3 - old
```

But we strongly recommend that you don't use complicated code. It would be clearer to use another variable to interchange the two values.

How about this guideline?

"Use comments to describe data items".

For example:

```
var
    x : integer ; { salary }
```

This is awful! Instead a meaningful name should have been used - without a comment like this:

```
var
    salary : integer ;
```

How about:

"Use comments to describe actions".

For example:

```
{ generate a random number in the range 0 to 1 }
r := random etc
```

Instead, why not use a procedure with a meaningful name:

```
generateRandom0Or1
```

Finally, maybe the best guideline is:

> Use comments sparingly and judiciously to describe something that we can't describe in the coding itself.

For example:

1. to state the overall purpose of the program;
2. when we can't describe what a procedure does by means of its name, because we only have a limited number of characters available;
3. to give the name of the author of the program and information about the modification history of the program.

## Blank lines and underlining comments

Look at this example:

```
program ...........

procedure ....
{-----------}
.............
..............

procedure .....
{------------}
..........
...........
..........

procedure ....
{-----------}
.............
..............
..........

begin
.............
..............
.............
end.
```

The comments underlining the procedure headings and the blank lines between the procedures emphasize the structure and enhance the readability.

## Summary

When used carefully, good names, indentation, blank lines, new pages and comments can considerably aid the clarity of a program and hence affect the ease with which the program can be checked, errors can be found and changes can be made.

## Exercise

Look at some of your earlier programs and ask yourself, "Are they readable?" If you can no longer understand them, how would someone else who had never seen them before?

# CHAPTER 12
# Debugging and testing

## Introduction

First let us try to define the terminology:

### Testing

means trying to demonstrate that a program works correctly by running it repeatedly with different test values.

### Bug

means an error in a program.

### Debugging

means locating and fixing the cause of errors.

Testing often reveals the presence of bugs, which then have to be debugged.

When we run a program, several things may happen:

1. **The program will not compile**.
   The compiler checks the syntax of the program and reveals errors such as semi-colons missing, misspelled names or variables that were not declared. The remedy is to consult the syntax diagrams and correct the errors.

2. **A run-time error occurs.**
   For example the program tries to divide by zero, or tries to read an integer and instead is given a character that is not a digit. In this situation a good system will tell us which program statement it was that caused the crash. Debugging is necessary.

3. **The program runs, but gives no output.**
   This is probably because it has gone into an endless loop. (A *while* statement whose condition is always met, so that the body is obeyed again and again). Debugging is necessary.

4. **The program runs, but gives wrong output.**
   Debugging is necessary.

5. **The program runs and gives correct output.**
   We must continue testing until we are convinced that it always will work correctly.

# Debugging (pinpointing and fixing bugs)

There are three main ways of locating bugs:

**Dry running** - we pretend to be a computer and work through the program, executing it;

**Tracing** - we use a system facility to see which statements are being executed and in what order. We can then check to see if the actual sequence is the same as the one we expect.

**Additional output** - we insert additional *write* statements into the program so that more information is available about what it is actually doing. When we insert these temporary *write* statements in the program, we should first pause and think about the best places to put them.

# A Case study in debugging

Look at the program , in chapter ten, that plays the game called "which hand". The program as shown compiles and runs. But, after we have played it for a while, we notice that apart from the first time we always lose! Then, when we have had enough, the program ends by saying that we got 298680 right guesses and 4 wrong!

Let's look into the problem about the totals first. There are two possibilities. Something is wrong with either the updating of the totals, or with the displaying of the totals. So we place *write* statements to display the values of the variables "wins" and "losses" immediately before and after the call on the procedure "updateTotals". When we do this, we see immediately that the initial values of "wins" and "losses" are not what we expect, and we realise that we have omitted to give them initial values of zero.

So we add a new procedure "initialiseTotals" and run the program again. This time we still keep losing the game, but at least the total scores are correct. We then place a *write* statement after the call on "invite" to display the values both of the computer's selection, "hand", and our guess, "guess". This shows that, although the value of "hand" is ok, the value of "reply" is a space. No wonder we always get it wrong! The cause of this error is more subtle than the last one. Because there is no *readln* after the *read* in procedure "decideWhatNext", the *read* in "invite" continues reading on the same line and reads the character after the "y". This is an end of line character, which is treated by Pascal as if it were a space. The remedy is to place a *readln* after the *read* in the procedure "invite".

There is still another bug in this program. Can you find it?

# Testing

Let us explore a series of possible approaches to testing. First, we might think of devising a *selection* of input data values and comparing the actual with the expected outcome. In this situation it might be best to ask someone other than the programmer to devise the data, so that any conscious or unconscious bias is avoided. A simple example illustrates the drawback of this approach. Here is the actual coding of a program whose stated purpose is to multiply two integers:

```
read (x, y) ;
product := x * y ;
if product = 42 then begin
     product := 0 end ;
write (product)
```

Use of selective test data will almost certainly fail to reveal this "bug". We might argue that the bug is obvious - but if we do, we do so on the basis *not* of testing the code but on the basis of inspecting it.

A second method of testing might be to use all possible input values, again checking for correct outcome. But even for a program to multiply two 32 bit integers this would take 50 billion years (assuming a 1 millisecond integer multiply instruction is provided by the hardware of the computer). So exhaustive testing is almost always impracticable.

A third method suggests itself following our experience with the first. We saw that we cannot realistically test a program by considering it merely as a "black box"; we can only test a program adequately using knowledge about its internal structure. So why not use test data that causes every program path to be executed in all possible combinations? But, again, this can be too lengthy a process for any but a small program.

Finally then we are led to the conclusion that the best we can do is to devise test data that causes execution of every program path (though not all combinations of paths), at least once in the testing. But unfortunately this is still far from fool-proof. Consider, for example:

```
read (x)
while more data do
     total := total + x
     read (x)
endwhile
write (total)
```

This will *sometimes* give the expected answer. Can you see why? (The answer is that the variable "total" has not been given an initial value).

Another view of testing is that we should make sure to test the actions that a program takes in special cases. For example, suppose we have a program that scans a file of records that describe people, and produces a list of those eligible to vote. The test data should describe people who are just below, just above and just equal to the critical age.

However much we test our programs, using all our skill and intuition, we can never be sure that we have eradicated all the faults. The situation is well summed up by Dijkstra's famous remark:

"Testing can only show the presence of bugs, never their absence".

The trouble is, of course, that bugs always surface at the worst possible time - for example when you are demonstrating a program to a client. This phenomenon has long been known to students of reliability, who quote Murphy's laws:

"If a system can fail, it will"

"- and at the worst possible moment".

In the real world, evidence of the limitations of testing software is there for all to see. More scientifically, in a carefully controlled experiment carried out in 1978, 59 people were asked to test a 63 line PL/1 program. The people were workers in the computer industry. Most of them were programmers. They had an average of 11 years experience in computing. They were told of a suspicion that the program was not perfect and asked to test the program until they felt that they had found all the errors (if any). An error meant a discrepancy between the program and the specification. The people were provided with the program specification, the program listing, a computer to run the program on, and as much time as they wanted. The mean number of bugs found was 5.7. The most errors any individual found was nine. The least any person found was three. The actual number of bugs was 15. There were four bugs that no-one found.

Additional findings were that the people were not careful enough in comparing the actual output from the program with the expected outcome. Bugs were missed in this way. Also the people spent too long on testing the normal conditions that the program had to encounter, rather than on testing special cases and invalid input situations.

## Summary

Testing is a poor technique. But until program proving becomes widely applicable it is a vital one. The best we can do is to select test data that:

(a) exercises all program paths

and

(b) tests actions that are taken in special cases.

# CHAPTER 13
# Systematic working

This chapter is essentially a lot of preaching and can therefore be a bit annoying to read. The ideas are based on the experiences of working programmers. But for people who regard programming as a fun activity, rather than as a job of work, they can seem restrictive. First let us review the stages of program development. They are:

    clarify the specification
    design
    check the design
    code
    check the code
    construct test data
    key in the program
    compile
    run
    compare actual with expected output
    debug.

This list draws attention to the fact that the act of writing a program (coding) is only a part of what's involved in developing a program. In fact a typical professional programmer spends only about 10% of his or her time on coding. The bulk of the time is spent on testing.

## Why design?

Compare developing a program with designing and building a bridge. We would not expect to see a bridge designer starting the design by thinking about the size of the rivets. Rather we would expect him or her to think about the grand structure of the bridge - whether it is to be a suspension bridge, for example. Similarly in program development, we might expect that the programmer would first think about the overall structure of the program, rather than think about the nature of fragments of code.

## Spend longer on design

Imagine two programmers working on the development of the same program. One doesn't believe in spending very long on design, or doesn't believe in design at all. He or she spends virtually no time on design, spends a fair time on coding and then goes on to start testing and debugging. Meanwhile the other, virtuous, programmer spends a long time on design and a little time on coding. Then, because the design of the program is sound, he or she completes testing and debugging smoothly and quickly - ahead of the other programmer. The programmer who didn't design may find serious design flaws during testing, which then consume a lot of time in re-writing big pieces of the program. It is far easier to correct design errors at an early stage - when all that is needed is an eraser, rather than later - when the program source must be changed and large parts of it might even have to be thrown away. Correcting design errors which survive until the program is in routine use all over the world will be more expensive still.

The moral is to spend longer on the design, resisting the urge to rush on to the coding - even when others are doing so. During design, try to discover alternative designs. Then decide between them, usually by choosing the simplest.

## The golden rule of programming

Since writing correct, maintainable programs is so difficult and time consuming, the golden rule is:

Only write new programs as a last resort.

Techniques used in industry for avoiding writing programs include:

modifying old designs and programs,
re-using procedures from old programs, and
re-using published code from books and journals.

You can use procedures from this book in some of the exercises.

# Don't be a terminal junky

A terminal junky is someone who enjoys spending hours at a terminal, playing games, debugging programs, sending messages to other people, and generally having a good time.

Firstly, there is usually a social reason for not doing this - there are far too few terminals for everyone to do this. But there is another good reason. The programmer who organises his or her time at the terminal will probably save time. Think of the situation. Terminal rooms are very often hot, noisy, and crowded. It is an unusual person who is not distracted by these things. Even when we have available our own personal computer, it is easy to waste a lot of time. So, here are some guidelines:

1.  Go to the terminal with a plan of what we are going to do.

2.  Don't spend time at the terminal experimenting (trying things that we have just thought of on the spur of the moment).

3.  Collect evidence of what has happened by the end of our session - an up-to-date listing of the program and the texts of messages output by our program and by the system.

4.  Retire somewhere quiet and peaceful and examine the evidence that we have collected.

Adopting these practices may well save us time. Time that we can then spend doing such fun things as ...

# Summary

If we are systematic, organised and self-disciplined we will probably save ourselves time.

# CHAPTER 14
# Arrays

Suppose we had to write a program to keep a count of the amount of rain which fell on the different days of the week throughout a year. Suppose also that the 365 rainfall figures were to be fed into the program, in no particular order, by typing two numbers: the first representing the day of the week and the second giving the rainfall for that day. We obviously need seven variables to represent the total rainfall for the seven days of the week. The pseudo-code for part of the design would look like this:

```
read (day, rain)
if day = 1 then
     total1 := total1 + rain
else
     if day = 2 then
          total2 := total2 + rain
     else
          if day = 3 then
               total3 := total3 + rain
          else
               if day = 4 then
                    total4 := total4 + rain
               else
                    if day = 5 then
                         total5 := total5 + rain
                    else
                         if day = 6 then
                              total6 := total6 + rain
                         else
                              total7 := total7 + rain
                         endif
                    endif
               endif
          endif
     endif
endif
```

You probably have something rather like this for dealing with the three piles in the program which plays the game of Nim.

Since the idea of computers should be to free people from boring repetitive tasks, we should look for a better solution whenever we are tempted to write anything like the above. Sometimes the better solution is to use procedures; in this case it is to use a kind of variable known as an array.

We often see data arranged as arrays in everyday life. Examples are:

> a bus timetable,
> a pools coupon,
> mathematical tables,
> a chess board.

What we now want to do is to create a whole array of integer variables to hold the seven rainfall totals. We might visualize them as looking like this in main memory:

120

```
total1 [          ]
total2 [          ]
total3 [          ]
total4 [          ]
total5 [          ]
total6 [          ]
total7 [          ]
```

We can declare such an array in Pascal like this:

```
var total : array [1..7] of integer ;
```

The name of the whole array is "total". It has 7 components in it. If we want to talk about a particular component in the array, say the 5th, we refer to it as total [5]. For example the value of the 5th component of "total" might be the number 67. Note that on some systems, the keyboards and printers don't have the [ and ] characters on them, and we then have to use (. and .) instead, respectively. We call the number that picks out the particular component of the array a *subscript* (5 in the above example).

The main advantage of the array if that it allows us to use the same piece of program to access *any* component of the array. We can, thereby, avoid repeating parts of a program's text. The fragment of pseudo-code at the start of the chapter can now be replaced with:

```
read (day, rain)
total [day] := total [day] + rain
```

Using an array has allowed us to replace the last 25 lines of the original algorithm with just one line! Notice that it is the value of the variable "day" which determines exactly which component of "total" will be changed. Each execution of the fragment changes only one component.

Some things that we might like to do with this array of rainfall data are:

calculate the total rainfall for the year
find the largest total
find the day with the largest total
change the values of the totals

Here is a fragment of program to calculate the year's total:

```
yearsTotal := 0 ;
for day := 1 to 7 do begin
    yearsTotal := yearsTotal + total [day] end
```

Note that *for* statements are frequently used in conjunction with arrays.

Here is a fragment of program to find the largest total:

```
largest := total [1] ;
for day := 2 to 7 do begin
    if total [day] > largest then begin
        largest := total [day] end end
```

You write the code to find the rainiest day.

Components of an array can be used wherever we can use an ordinary variable. For example, here is fragment which would replace the totals with values from the keyboard:

```
for day := 1 to 7 do begin
    read (total [day]) end
```

## Subscripts

Subscripts don't have to start at the value 1. We could have decided to number the days in the week from 0 to 6, or in any other way. For example:

```
var total : array [0..6] of integer ;
```

but subscript values do have to be integers and go up in steps of one.

## Arrays of characters

Arrays of characters are useful for holding words or names. Here is an example which inputs a name from the keyboard and replies with a friendly message:

```
program friend1 (input, output) ;
var
      name       : array [1..10] of char ;
      singleChar : char ;
      position   : integer ;

begin

position := 1 ;
read (singleChar) ;
while singleChar <> ' ' do begin
    name [position] := singleChar ;
    position := position + 1 ;
    read (singleChar) end ;
name [position] := ' ' ;

write ('hello ') ;

position := 1 ;
while name [Position] <> ' ' do begin
    write ( name [position] ) ;
    position := position + 1 end ;

writeln

end.
```

## Exceeding the declared size of an array

In the above example, if the name of the person was longer than 10 characters, a run-time error would occur. A good system would display a message like this:

"High bound checking error at statement 4 in the main program".

Low bound and high bound are the technical terms for the lowest and highest subscripts of an array. So this message simply means that if the program had been allowed to continue, it would have accessed a non-existent component above the maximum for the array in question. The program won't deal with longer names, unless we alter the declaration of variable "name" so that it has more components in it. In Pascal we always have to say how long an array is. So in the above program, it would be best to write in a check to ensure that a name is, in fact, no longer than 10 characters.

# Arrays as parameters

The last example program would have been better if we had used two procedures, like this:

```
program friend2 (input, output) ;
var
     name : array [1..10] of char ;

procedure readWord
{----------------}
     (var word : array [low .. high : integer] of char) ;
var
     position   : integer ;
     singleChar : char ;
begin
position := low ;                              { see below }
read (singleChar) ;
while singleChar <> ' ' do begin
     word [position] := singleChar ;
     position := position + 1 ;
     read (singleChar) end ;
word [position] := ' ' ;
end ;

procedure writeWord
{----------------}
     (var word : array [low .. high : integer] of char) ;
var
     position : integer ;
begin
position := low ;                              { see below }
while word [Position] <> ' '  do begin
     write ( word [position] ) ;
     position := position + 1 end ;
end ;

begin
readWord (name) ;
write ('Hello ') ;
writeWord (name) ;
writeln
end.
```

When we declare a parameter in a procedure heading, we have to give the type of the parameter; for example, whether it is integer or char. The position is a little more complicated with array parameters because there is no single word for the type. Instead we have to describe the array in the procedure heading itself, as we

124

did in the above program. The only differences between this description and an ordinary array variable declaration are:

1. we have to give names to the lowest and highest subscripts rather than specifying their values, and

2. we have to specify that the subscripts are integers. This is done as shown in the example above.

The names we have to give to the lowest and highest subscripts behave as if they were local variables which are automatically given the values of the size of the array when they are created, that is when the procedure is entered. This is why we were able to refer to them in the procedures, at the points indicated by the comments. This facility is actually very useful. It means that we can change programs to use different-sized arrays, without having to make any changes to the array-handling procedures. It also means that the procedures can deal with arrays with any range of subscripts; for instance, an array with subscripts zero to nine, or from two to fifty.

## A possible problem

There is a problem with many current versions of Pascal: they do not allow array parameter declarations in procedure headings, as we have just described. Such parameters are known as *conformant arrays*. Find out whether your system allows them; if it does, you can skip this section; if not, read on.

With a system without conformant arrays, there is no problem when we *call* a procedure giving an array as a parameter. But the Pascal compiler won't allow arrays to be declared in procedure headings as in the above example.

The way round this nuisance is to declare something called a "type" at the top of the program. Amongst other things, a type is a way of giving a name to the size and component type of an array. For example:

```
type
      wordType  = array [1..10] of char ;
```

Declarations like this are written at the top of the program, after the program header, but before variable declarations. Their syntax is shown by these diagrams:

## Program

```
────→ program ────→ NAME ────→ (input, output) ; ─┐
        ┌──────────────────────────←───────────────┘
        │  ┌──────→ TYPE DECLARATIONS ──────┐
        │  └───────────────←────────────────┘
        │  ┌──────→ VARIABLE DECLARATIONS ──────┐
        │  └───────────────←────────────────────┘
        │  ┌──────→ PROCEDURE DECLARATION ──────┐
        │  └───────────────←────────────────────┘
        └──────→ begin ──→ STATEMENT ──→ end. ────→
                     └──────── ; ←──────┘
```

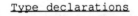
## Type declarations

```
→ type ─┬→ NAME → = array [ → RANGE → ] of → TYPE → ; ─┬→
        └──────────────────←───────────────────────────┘
```

## Range

```
────→ INTEGER ────→ .. ───→ INTEGER ────→
```

## Type

```
──────┬───→ integer ───┬──────→
      ├───→ char ───────┤
      └───→ TYPENAME ───┘
```

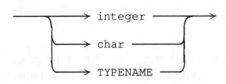

A "typename" is simply a name that has been used in a type declaration.

Using type declarations, the problem is solved and we can now write the program in this way:

```pascal
program friend3 (input, output) ;
type
     wordType  = array [1..10] of char ;

var
     name : wordType ;

procedure readWord (var word : wordType) ;
{-----------------------------------------}
var
     position   : integer ;
     singleChar : char ;
begin
position := 1 ;
read (singleChar) ;
while singleChar <> ' ' do begin
     word [position] := singleChar ;
     position := position + 1 ;
     read (singleChar) end ;
word [position] := ' ' ;
end ;

procedure writeWord (var word : wordType) ;
{-----------------------------------------}
var
     position : integer ;
begin
position := 1 ;
while word [Position] <> ' '  do begin
     write ( word [position] ) ;
     position := position + 1 end ;
end ;

begin
readWord (name) ;
write ('Hello ') ;
writeWord (name) ;
writeln
end.
```

There are three things to note about this. Firstly, the convention of choosing names of types so that they end in "Type", as in "wordType", is used so that we do not have to tax our powers of invention by making up two names for similar things. Secondly, the procedures will only work on variables of type "wordType": if "name" had been declared like this:

```
program friend3 (input, output) ;
type
     wordType  = array [1..10] of char ;
var
     name : array [1..10] of char ;
```

or like this:

```
program friend3 (input, output) ;
type
     wordType  = array [1..10] of char ;
     otherType = array [1..10] of char ;
var
     name : otherType ;
```

the program would not compile. This is because the variable "name" would not be regarded as being of the *same* type as "wordType", which the procedures are expecting. Lastly, notice that the lower bound for the arrays has had to be fixed at one, in the procedures.

# Revised syntax diagrams

These diagrams cover array variable declarations and array parameters:

Variable declarations

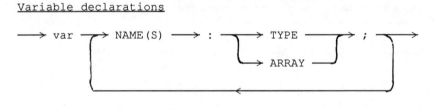

Name(s)

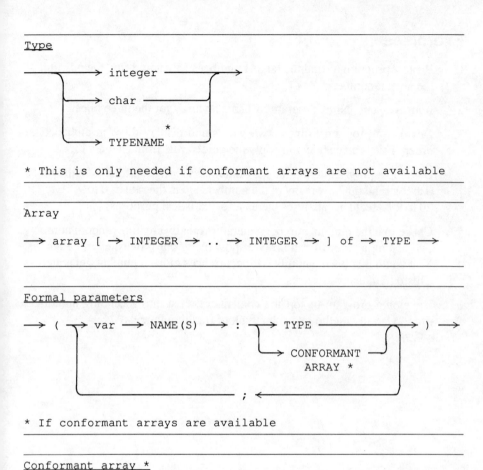

Type

integer

char

*
TYPENAME

* This is only needed if conformant arrays are not available

Array

→ array [ → INTEGER → .. → INTEGER → ] of → TYPE →

Formal parameters

→ ( → var → NAME(S) → : → TYPE → ) →

CONFORMANT
ARRAY *

;

* If conformant arrays are available

Conformant array *

→ array [ → NAME → .. → NAME : integer → ] of → TYPE →

* If conformant arrays are available

## Summary

We use arrays to hold tables. They help us to avoid repeating similar pieces of program. Conformant arrays are the simplest way of passing arrays to procedures; if we do not have conformant arrays we have to use *types* instead.

# Exercises

1. Write a program to find the largest number in a list and find the *position* of the largest number.

2. Improve your "Nim" program by using an array for the three piles.

3. Develop a program to input two words and display them in alphabetical order. This is an easy if you apply the golden rule from chapter 13.

4. Develop a program to input a set of numbers, each of which is in the range 0 to 99. Find out how many of the numbers are in the ranges 0 to 9, 10 to 19, 20 to 29, etc. (This analyses the data for statistical purposes).

5. Check that the random number generator is really creating random numbers by keeping a record in an array of how many ones, twos, etc it generates. You could display the number of occurrences of each number generated as a histogram using asterisks.

6. Develop a program to sort the contents of a list into ascending numerical order. Use any method you can think of (nothing fancy!).

# CHAPTER 15
# More on arrays

## Searching and lookup

Consider this problem. A company employs a number of people. It wants a computer program to keep a record of its employees' dates of birth. Like most companies, it gives each employee a number. These numbers can be anything - they don't start at one and run up to some maximum value.

We could maintain a table with all the employee numbers in it. We can imagine it as looking like this in main memory:

| | | |
|---|---|---|
| [1] | 129 | employee |
| [2] | 7 | |
| [3] | 16 | |
| [4] | 850 | |
| [5] | 92 | |
| [6] | 385 | |
| etc | | |

and we could declare it in Pascal like this:

```
var  employee : array [1..100] of integer ;
```

Suppose we set up a second table with each person's year of birth in it. Let us ensure that entries correspond; so that, for example, for employee number 16, the number 16 is in the third component of the array "employee" and his or her year of birth is in the third component of an array "year". Here is the declaration for the other array:

```
var  year : array [1..100] of integer ;
```

it looks like this as a diagram:

```
[1]    1947        rain

[2]    1963

[3]    1921

[4]    1975

[5]    1969

[6]    1938

etc
```

To find the year of birth of an employee we need first to search table "employee" for the employee number. Then we can look in the corresponding component of "year". The algorithm is:

```
find (employee, number, position)
look up (year, position)
```

The algorithm for searching is:

```
find (employee, wanted, position)

    position := 1
    while employee [position] <> wanted do
        position := position + 1
    endwhile
```

The program fragment for looking up is :

```
write (year[position])
```

It is left to the reader to extend this algorithm so that it provides the day and month of birth (as numbers) as well as the year of birth.

It should be further extended so that it does something useful if the required employee number is not in the table. As it is, it would run until the Pascal system detected a run-time error.

These algorithms and programs for searching and lookup are frequently used, so it is worth spending the time to sort them out.

## Two-dimensional arrays

Let us extend the example we had in the previous chapter, where we had a week's worth of data on rainfall. Suppose we wanted to represent the rainfall for a four week period. As a diagram it might look like this:

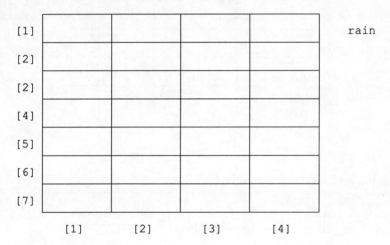

We could declare this in Pascal like this:

```
var   rain : array [1..7, 1..4] of integer ;
```

We would, for example, refer to the rainfall for the sixth day of week three as rain [6, 3]. It sometimes helps, in understanding, to view the first subscript as the row number and the second as the column number. Arrays with more than one dimension are covered in the syntax diagrams at the end of this book.

As another example, if we wanted to represent a chess board, eight squares by eight, we would want a two-dimensional array. This shows how we would declare one:

```
var  board : array [1..8, 1..8] of integer ;
```

If we wanted to specify a position, we could write:

```
board [2, 3] := 1
```

where 1 might be the code we have chosen to represent a pawn.

We might also use a two-dimensional array to "humanize" the problem above about employee records. Instead of calling people by numbers, we might want to store their names in the computer in an array that looks like this:

|      | [1] | [2] | [3] | [4] | [5] | [6] | [7] | [8] | [9] |        |
|------|-----|-----|-----|-----|-----|-----|-----|-----|-----|--------|
| [1]  | B   | i   | l   | l   |     |     |     |     |     | person |
| [2]  | M   | e   | g   |     |     |     |     |     |     |        |
| [3]  | A   | l   | e   | x   | a   | n   | d   | r   | a   |        |
| etc  |     |     |     |     |     |     |     |     |     |        |

This is the declaration for the table:

```
var  person : array [1..100, 1..9] of char ;
```

We could put values into the array like this:

```
person [2, 1] := 'M' ;
person [2, 2] := 'e' ;
person [2, 3] := 'g' ;
for column := 4 to 9 do begin
     person [2, column] := ' ' end ;
etc
```

Notice that we have to pad out short names with spaces to make them all the same length.

If we want to find a name in this table, the pseudo-code looks like this:

```
    row := 1
    while name not found do
        match := yes
        for column := 1 to 9 do
            if characters do not match then
                match := no
            endif
        endfor
        if match = yes then
            found := yes
        else
            row := row + 1
        endif
    endwhile
```

Notice that this only works if the name sought is in the table. Also note that it only works if the name sought matches exactly a name in the table - including spaces. It is left as an exercise for the reader to modify the algorithm so that it doesn't suffer from these drawbacks.

The Pascal code for the procedure "search" looks like this:

```
procedure search
{--------------}
  (var wanted: array [wantedLo  ..wantedHi  : integer] of char;
   var names : array [namesRowLo..namesRowHi: integer ;
                      namesColLo..namesColHi: integer] of char;
   var row    : integer) ;
var
     found, match : char ;
     column        : integer ;
begin
found := 'n' ;
row := namesRowLo ;
while found = 'n' do begin
     match := 'y' ;
     for column := wantedLo to wantedHi do begin
          if wanted[column] <> names[row, column] then begin
               match := 'n' end end ;
     if match = 'y' then begin
          found := 'y' end
     else begin
          row := row + 1 end end
end ;
```

Or, using type declarations:

```
program lookUp (input, output) ;
type
     wantedType = array [1..9] of char ;
     personType = array [1..100, 1..9] of char ;
var
     person   : personType ;
     wanted   : wantedType ;
     position : integer ;

procedure search
{--------------}
   (var wanted : wantedType ;
    var names  : personType ;
    var row    : integer) ;
var
     found, match : char ;
     column       : integer ;
begin
found := 'n' ;
row := 1 ;
while found = 'n' do begin
     match := 'y' ;
     for column := 1 to 9 do begin
          if wanted[column] <> names[row, column] then begin
               match := 'n' end end ;
     if match = 'y' then begin
          found := 'y' end
     else begin
          row := row + 1 end end
end ;
etc
```

## Arrays of arrays

You may consider that the two-dimensional array, to hold the people's names, is unnatural. What we really need is an array of names, where a name is an array of characters. Conveniently, in Pascal, a multi-dimensional array is considered to be an array of arrays. For example, the following declarations are identical:

```
var
     person : array [1..100, 1..9] of char ;
     person : array [1..100] of array [1..9] of char ;
```

The advantage of this is that with either of the above declarations, this fragment:

```
person [2]
```

refers to all nine characters of the second name.

Because of this, we can structure the "search" algorithm in this more natural way:

```
search table of names (wanted, names, row)

    row := 1
    while name not found do
        compare (wanted, names[row], match)
        if match = yes then
            found := yes
        else
            row := row + 1
        endif
    endwhile

compare (name1, name2, result)

    result:= yes
    for letter := 1 to 9 do
        if name1 [letter] <> name2 [letter] then
            result:= no
        endif
    endfor
```

Here it is in Pascal:

```pascal
procedure compare
{---------------}
   (var name1, name2
              : array [nameLo .. nameHi : integer] of char ;
    var result : char) ;
var
      letter : integer ;
begin
result:= 'y' ;
for letter := nameLo to nameHi do begin
      if name1 [letter] <> name2 [letter] then begin
          result := 'n' end end
end ;


procedure search
{--------------}
  (var wanted: array [wantedLo  ..wantedHi  : integer] of char;
   var names : array [namesRowLo..namesRowHi: integer] of
              array [namesColLo..namesColHi: integer] of char;
   var row    : integer) ;
var
      found, match : char ;
      column        : integer ;
begin
found := 'n' ;
row := namesRowLo ;   { see below }
while found = 'n' do begin
      compare (wanted, names[row], match) ;
      if match = 'y' then begin
          found := 'y' end
      else begin
          row := row + 1 end end
end ;
```

Notice that the "search" procedure passes whole names (which are arrays) to the "compare" procedure. The result is smaller, clearer procedures.

If your system does not support conformant arrays, or if it does not treat multi-dimensional arrays as arrays of arrays, you can achieve the same effect by using types:

```
program lookUp (input, output) ;
type
     nameType   = array [1..9] of char ;
     personType = array [1..100] of nameType ;
var
     person   : personType ;
     wanted   : nameType ;
     position : integer ;

procedure compare
{--------------}
   (var name1, name2  : nameType ; var result : char) ;
var
     letter : integer ;
begin
result:= 'y' ;
for letter := 1 to 9 do begin
     if name1 [letter] <> name2 [letter] then begin
          result := 'n' end end
end ;

procedure search (var wanted : nameType ;
{--------------------------------------}
                    var names  : personType ;
                    var row    : integer) ;
var
     found, match : char ;
     column       : integer ;
begin
found := 'n' ;
row := 1 ;
while found = 'n' do begin
     compare (wanted, names[row], match) ;
     if match = 'y' then begin
          found := 'y' end
     else begin
          row := row + 1 end end
end ;
etc
```

A call to the "search" procedure in all the above versions looks like this:

```
search (wanted, person, position)
```

# Multi-dimensional arrays

Two isn't the limit for the number of dimensions of arrays. In fact you can have as many as you need to match your problem. As an example, consider collecting rainfall data for each day in the week, for each week in the month, for each month in the year, and for each year in the decade. We would need a 4-dimensional array:

```
var  rain : array [1..7, 1..4, 1..12, 1980..1989] ;
```

As an another example, if you wanted to represent cars in a multi-storey car park, you could use a 3 dimensional array.

# Summary

Two-dimensional arrays are useful for representing two dimensional tables and lists of words. We can use more than two dimensions if we need.

# Exercises

1.  Write a procedure to store a list of words. Write a second procedure to print out the list. Use the procedures together in a program to test them. Hint: the "readWord" and "writeWord" procedures from the previous chapter should be useful.

2.  Write a program to read a date in the form 5 11 47 and display it in the form: 5 November 47. Hint: the procedure from the first exercise should be used to set up a list of month names.

3.  Modify the calculator program from chapter nine so that it accepts input like this:

    23 plus 78 minus 45 times 2 equals

    but this time, make it check that the operators are spelled correctly.

4.  Play battleships.

5.  (For the mathematically minded), multiply two matrices  together.

# CHAPTER 16
# Real numbers

In Pascal, we can declare variables to hold real numbers. (Real numbers are numbers with fractional parts). Variables for real numbers are declared in just the same manner as integer ones except that the word *real* is used instead of *integer*. The operators +, −, /, and * are used to describe addition, subtraction, division, and multiplication respectively. Brackets must be used wherever necessary to clarify any possible ambiguity.

Here is an example which uses *real* variables to calculate the area of a triangle:

```
program triangleArea (input, output) ;
var
     area, base, height : real ;
begin
base := 2.3 ;
height := 2.6 ;
area := 0.5 * base * height ;
etc
```

Here is another, it calculates the volume of a sphere:

```
program sphereVolume (input, output) ;
var
     volume, radius, pi : real ;
begin
radius := 1.5 ;
pi := 3.142 ;
volume := (4/3) * pi * radius * radius * radius ;
etc
```

141

Several mathematical functions are provided in Pascal:

| | |
|---|---|
| sin (x) | x must be in radians |
| cos (x) | x must be in radians |
| exp (x) | e to the power x |
| ln (x) | log base e of x |
| sqrt (x) | square root of x |
| arctan (x) | angle whose tan is x |
| abs (x) | abs (x) and abs (–x) are both x |
| sqr (x) | square of x |

Both *abs* and *sqr* provide integer results with integer quantities and real results with real quantities.

Here is an example which shows the use of a function in calculating the area of any triangle:

```
halfSum := (a + b + c) / 2 ;
area := sqrt (halfSum*(halfSum-a)*(halfSum-b)*(halfSum-c)) ;
```

A useful function that is missing from Pascal is the facility to raise any number to any power. But this can be done by using the formula:

x to the power p = exp(p ln(x))

## When do we use integers and reals?

In a sense, real variables are more useful than integer because we can do division "properly" and because several standard functions are available. So why have integers? The main answer is that we use whichever type of data best fits the problem we have to solve. If we are calculating the volume of a sphere - use reals. If we are counting sheep - use integers.

There are particular situations where only an integer will do. One we have already met - integers are always used for bank accounts. The other is array subscripts. The Pascal rules, quite reasonably, insist that an array subscript must be an integer.

Precision is another factor in assessing whether to use real or integer. Integers are represented *exactly* in a computer, but reals are often *approximated* with a precision of say 6 significant figures. (Find out how many it is on your computer). This approximation can be quite striking. Run a program that inputs a real number and immediately outputs it. Give it some data and see what happens. Every so often you will enter a value that is represented inside the computer in an approximate way. Therefore, when it is output, its value will have mysteriously changed somewhat.

Range is the complement of precision. In most computers, only a limited range of integers is allowed. (Find out what the range is on your computer). In contrast the range of possible values for reals is, on most computers, enormously greater.

Finally program performance can affect the choice. Usually a program that uses integers will be smaller and run faster than the same program using reals.

In summary, the choice of real or integer to represent a data item depends on:

> the nature of the information being represented (particularly
> range,                                                    array subscripts),
> precision,
> performance.

## Mixing reals and integers (careful!)

Pascal is usually very scrupulous about mixing data with different types - it doesn't normally allow it. For example it doesn't allow arithmetic to be done on characters. Mixing reals and integers is the single exception. It requires special care. The rules are:

1.  If a statement has *any* real quantities in it, then *every* piece of the statement is treated as real. For example:

```
var
      r : real ;
begin
r := 6.2 / 10 ;
r := 7 / 62 ;
```

and the example already shown above:

```
volume := (4/3) * pi * radius * radius * radius ;
```

2. It is forbidden to have an integer on the left hand side and a real on the right hand side of an assignment. For example:

```
var
      i : integer ;
begin
i := 6.2        { error }
```

is illegal.

Very occasionally, we have a real value that we want to convert to an integer. For this purpose, two special functions, *trunc* and *round*, are provided. Here is an example which demonstrates their use:

```
var
      i : integer ;
      r : real ;
begin
r := 1.6 ;
i := trunc (r) ;
write (i) ;
i := round (r) ;
write (i) ;
```

It would give the following output:

```
        1        2
```

*Trunc* discards the fractional part of the number, that is it truncates it and converts it to an integer. *Round* changes the number to to the *nearest* integer.

## Summary

In Pascal, real numbers and integers are both available; care is needed in mixing them.

Pascal has several mathematical functions.

# Exercises

1.  Calculate the mean of a set of numbers that are keyed in as data.

2.  Find the sum of the series:

    $1 + 1/2 + 1/3 + 1/4 \dots$

    until a term less than 0.001 is reached.

3.  Calculate the roots of a quadratic equation according to the well known formula.

4.  Write a program to calculate pi using the following formula:

    $pi/4 = 1 - 1/3 + 1/5 - 1/7 + 1/9 \dots$

5.  Using *real* arithmetic, calculate the compound interest on £100 invested at 12% for six years. Compare the answer with the one you got in chapter eight.

# CHAPTER 17
# Top-Down Implementation

A common development path is to design a complete program, code it, key it in, and test it. A possible problem with this approach is that we are running a complete program for the first time *in its entirety*. Locating bugs in such a situation can be very difficult, particularly, of course, if the program is large. Even getting a "clean" compilation can be difficult, if things are done in this way. It might be better if we could tackle the testing and debugging of a program using only small pieces at a time. We could start with one piece, test it until we were satisfied with it, add a new piece, test it, and so on. One way of doing this is called Top-Down Implementation.

Top-down implementation proceeds like this. We design and code the complete program as before. Then we take the "top-most" part of the program - the main program - and test it on its own. What about the procedures used? For these we temporarily substitute (almost) empty procedures, called "stubs". A stub might:

1.  do nothing at all,
2.  display a message to demonstrate that it has been executed, or
3.  carry out a pale imitation of the procedure's full task.

Having tested the main program in this way, the next step is to replace just one of the stubs with its real version. Once again, any procedures that are used appear as mere stubs. The program is again tested in this state. The process continues in this way, replacing one stub at a time by the real procedure and testing the program in its incomplete form.

The beauty of this method is that if the program fails to compile after a bit has been added, the fault is almost certainly in the new part. Similarly, if the program contains an error the place to look for the bug is in that same new part. The effect of using top-down implementation is to reduce the problem of debugging a program to that of debugging a lot of smaller ones - which is easier.

## Case study

Remember the program to play the game of which hand? Here it is at the first stage in development according to top-down implementation. All the program has been coded, but only a part of it has been keyed into the computer. Missing procedures have been replaced by stubs. The program will run and can be tested (up to a point) in this form.

```
program whichHand1 (input, output) ;
var
     random, wins, losses : integer ;
     moreGames              : char ;

procedure playAGame (var random, wins, losses : integer) ;
{------------------------------------------------------------}
begin
write ('playing a game') ;
writeln
end ;

procedure decideWhatNext (var reply : char) ;
{------------------------------------------------}
begin
reply := 'n'
end ;

procedure displayTotals (var wins, losses : integer) ;
{-----------------------------------------------------}
begin
write ('displaying totals') ;
writeln
end ;

procedure getSeed (var random : integer) ;
{-------------------------------------------}
begin
write ('getting first random number') ;
writeln
end ;

begin
getSeed (random) ;
moreGames := 'y' ;
while moreGames = 'y' do begin
     playAGame (random, wins, losses) ;
     decideWhatNext (moreGames) end ;
displayTotals (wins, losses)
end.
```

The stub procedures are mainly of the second type listed above - they just display a message to indicate that they have been executed. The procedure "decideWhatNext" is of the third type - it carries out a pale imitation of its full task. The main program, however, has been typed in full. This version of the program does not expect any input. When it is executed, its output is as follows:

```
getting first random number
playing a game
displaying totals
```

which is exactly as we expected it would be. The main result of this test is that we can see that the variables are correctly declared, that the formal and actual parameters of the procedures are in agreement and that the main program is correct so far.

Next we replace the stub "decideWhatNext" with the following:

```
procedure decideWhatNext (var reply : char) ;
{---------------------------------------------}
begin
write ('Do you wish to play again?') ;
writeln ;
read (reply) ;
while (reply <> 'y') and (reply <> 'n') do begin
     write ('Please answer y or n') ;
     writeln ;
     read (reply) ;
     readln end
end ;
```

This time, when the program is executed with some correct test data, we get this unexpected result:

```
getting first random number
playing a game
Do you wish to play again?
y
playing a game
Do you wish to play again?
Please answer y or n
y
playing a game
Do you wish to play again?
n
displaying totals
```

The program does not always wait for us to say whether we want to play again. The problem must be in the procedure we just inserted. In fact it the missing *readln* statement discussed in chapter twelve. We insert the missing statement and retest the program, this time the output is correct:

```
getting first random number
playing a game
Do you wish to play again?
y
playing a game
Do you wish to play again?
x
Please answer y or n
x
Please answer y or n
y
playing a game
Do you wish to play again?
n
displaying totals
```

Next we replace the stub "displayTotals" with this:

```
procedure displayTotals (var wins, losses : integer) ;
{-----------------------------------------------------}
begin
write ('You won ', wins, ' game(s) and lost ') ;
write (losses, ' game(s)') ;
writeln ;
write ('Goodbye  - thankyou for playing') ;
writeln
end ;
```

And get this result:

```
getting first random number
playing a game
Do you wish to play again?
n
You won       298680 game(s) and lost          -2 game(s)
Goodbye  - thankyou for playing
```

The strange totals are caused by our failure to initialise the wins and losses, so we insert this procedure:

```
procedure initialiseTotals (var wins, losses : integer) ;
{--------------------------------------------------------}
begin
wins := 0 ;
losses := 0
end ;
```

We add a call to the new procedure to the main program and repeat the above test. But this time, because we have altered the main program, we have to choose test data which will re-test the main program as well. The output produced by the program is now:

```
getting first random number
playing a game
Do you wish to play again?
y
playing a game
Do you wish to play again?
n
You won              0 game(s) and lost              0 game(s)
Goodbye  - thankyou for playing
```

Next we add the following:

```
procedure choose (var random : integer ; var hand : char) ;
{------------------------------------------------------------}
begin
write ('choosing a hand') ;
writeln
end ;

procedure invite (var guess : char) ;
{---------------------------------}
begin
write ('inviting a guess') ;
writeln
end ;

procedure displayAppropriateMessage (var guess, hand : char) ;
{------------------------------------------------------------}
begin
write ('displaying appropriate message') ;
writeln
end ;

procedure updateTotals (var wins, losses : integer ;
{-------------------------------------------------}
                             var guess, hand : char) ;
begin
write ('updating totals') ;
writeln
end ;

procedure playAGame (var random, wins, losses : integer) ;
{--------------------------------------------------------}
var
    hand, guess : char ;
begin
choose (random, hand) ;
invite (guess) ;
displayAppropriateMessage (guess, hand) ;
updateTotals (wins, losses, guess, hand)
end ;

procedure getSeed (var random : integer) ;
{----------------------------------------}
begin
random := 12345
end ;
```

Note that the first four procedures are new stubs, the other two are full versions of existing stubs. Now, when we execute the program we get:

```
choosing a hand
inviting a guess
displaying appropriate message
updating totals
Do you wish to play again?
n
You won                 0 game(s) and lost               0 game(s)
Goodbye  - thankyou for playing
```

This is as we expected it to be. Notice that since we had not altered any other parts of the program, there was no need to repeat any of the previous testing.

Now we try adding these replacement procedures:

```
procedure choose (var random : integer ; var hand : char) ;
{------------------------------------------------------------}
begin
hand := 'l'
end ;

procedure invite (var guess : char) ;
{-----------------------------------}
begin
write ('Choose a hand (l or r)') ;
writeln ;
read (guess) ;
readln ;
while (guess <> 'l') and (guess <> 'r') do begin
     write ('Please answer l or r') ;
     writeln ;
     read (guess) ;
     readln end
end ;
```

Note that the effect of the watered-down "choose" procedure is to make testing much simpler, as we can now tell which of our guesses should be correct.

This time we get this output:

```
Choose a hand (l or r)
x
Please answer l or r
x
Please answer l or r
l
displaying appropriate message
updating totals
Do you wish to play again?
n
You won            0 game(s) and lost            0 game(s)
Goodbye  - thankyou for playing
```

This is also as we would expect it to be.

We now add this replacement procedure:

```
procedure updateTotals (var wins, losses : integer ;
{-----------------------------------------------------}
                        var guess, hand  : char) ;
begin
if guess = hand then begin
    wins := wins + 1 end
else begin
    losses := losses + 1 end
end ;
```

The output produced by the program is then:

```
Choose a hand (l or r)
l
displaying appropriate message
Do you wish to play again?
y
Choose a hand (l or r)
l
displaying appropriate message
Do you wish to play again?
y
Choose a hand (l or r)
r
displaying appropriate message
Do you wish to play again?
n
You won            2 game(s) and lost            1 game(s)
Goodbye  - thankyou for playing
```

Because that is correct, we can proceed to add the following replacement procedure:

```
procedure displayAppropriateMessage (var guess, hand : char) ;
{-------------------------------------------------------------}
begin
if guess = hand then begin
     write ('Correct') end
else begin
     write ('Wrong') end ;
writeln
end ;
```

This is the output produced by that version of the program:

```
Choose a hand (l or r)
l
Correct
Do you wish to play again?
y
Choose a hand (l or r)
l
Correct
Do you wish to play again?
y
Choose a hand (l or r)
r
Wrong
Do you wish to play again?
n
You won              2 game(s) and lost            1 game(s)
Goodbye  - thankyou for playing
```

Lastly, we can begin to add the code which makes the computer choose "randomly". Here is the first attempt at it:

```
procedure getNext (var random : integer) ;
{----------------------------------------}
begin
write ('getting next random number') ;
writeln
end ;


procedure choose (var random : integer ; var hand : char) ;
{----------------------------------------------------------}
var
      random0Or1 : integer ;
begin
random0Or1 := 0 ;
getNext (random) ;
if random0Or1 = 0 then begin
      hand := 'l' end
else begin
      hand := 'r' end
end ;
```

Here is the output:

```
getting next random number
Choose a hand (l or r)
l
Correct
Do you wish to play again?
n
You won            1 game(s) and lost            0 game(s)
Goodbye  - thankyou for playing
```

It is correct. Before adding the final missing parts, we change the first statement of the procedure "choose" to assign a value of one rather then zero and then we get this output from the program:

```
getting next random number
Choose a hand (l or r)
l
Wrong
Do you wish to play again?
n
You won            0 game(s) and lost            1 game(s)
Goodbye  - thankyou for playing
```

Which is also as it should be.

Lastly, we add these replacement procedures to complete the program:

```
procedure getNext (var random : integer) ;
{----------------------------------------}
begin
random := ((random * 25173) + 13849) mod 65536
end ;


procedure choose (var random : integer ; var hand : char) ;
{----------------------------------------------------------}
var
      random0Or1 : integer ;
begin
random0Or1 := random div (65536 div 3) ;
getNext (random) ;
if random0Or1 = 0 then begin
      hand := 'l' end
else begin
      hand := 'r' end
end ;
```

Here is the output from the final version of the program:

```
Choose a hand (l or r)
r
Wrong
Do you wish to play again?
y
Choose a hand (l or r)
r
Wrong
Do you wish to play again?
y
Choose a hand (l or r)
r
Wrong
Do you wish to play again?
y
Choose a hand (l or r)
r
Wrong
Do you wish to play again?
y
Choose a hand (l or r)
r
Correct
Do you wish to play again?
n
You won              1 game(s) and lost          4 game(s)
Goodbye  - thankyou for playing
```

Apart from the fact that we appear to be rather unlucky with our guesses, the output is as we would expect.

## Discussion

The errors in the program were easier to find using top-down implementation, than by testing the complete program. Also, using top-down implementation, the program has been more thoroughly tested, without a great deal of extra effort compared with when we first tested it.

Top-down implementation has the advantage that we are only testing a small piece of the program at a time, using the existing, tested part of the program as a "test bed". So most of the time the cause of an error will be the procedure that has just been incorporated.

Another, major advantage of the method is that if there were a serious design fault, it would be probably be found at an early stage in testing; and could therefore be corrected without the effort of changing code which had been entered into the computer. Major design errors are more likely in the top levels of the design and these are the ones that are implemented first.

A slight disadvantage of the method is that the stubs may contain statements that are later deleted. These are only small bits of program, however, and the effort of writing them compares favourably with the effort of inserting additional *write* statements in a large, complete but incorrect program.

As we saw in chapter twelve, no method of testing is perfect and top-down implementation is no exception - there is still an error in the program.

## Summary

Top-down implementation makes testing easier. It has the advantage that design faults are found as soon as possible.

# CHAPTER 18
# File handling

Information is usually stored on backing store for the following two main reasons:

1.   because there is too much information to hold in main memory, or

2.   because the information must be passed from one program to another.

The tax details about the population of a country is an example of the first case. It is unlikely that all the details of all the people would fit into the main memory at once, nor is it necessary. Pascal programs are an example of the second case. They are passed from the text editor to the compiler, which are themselves both programs.

Information can be recorded on backing-store devices (magnetic tape or disc) just like music can be recorded and played back from a domestic tape recorder. Information held on backing store is said to be held in files. Usually a single file holds pieces of information that are related. Examples are:
>    a single program,
>    a list of names and addresses,
>    last week's sales figures,
>    the results of a survey,
>    some data from an experiment.

We can give files names; usually we choose descriptive ones. The rules for file names differ from one computer system to another, so you will need to know what form the name of a file can take on your computer system.

In order to access files, Pascal programs use the *read* and *write* statements. *Read* inputs data from a file into main memory. *Write* outputs data from main memory to a file.

Using Pascal, the only type of file that can be manipulated is called a serial (sometimes sequential) file. A serial file has the following, significant characteristics:

1.  It can only be read by starting at the beginning and reading data items one by one until the end of the file is reached. (We can't go backwards and forwards just as we like).

2.  The only way we can write new information to a file is to re-create it from nothing by writing new data, starting at the beginning and continuing serially until all the information is written.

These rules are crucial and it is vital to understand them. Note that one implication is that it is impossible to add new information to the end of an existing file. Even more important, *it is impossible to change the contents of a file.* The only way to change information or add to information held in a file is to serially create a copy incorporating all the desired changes.

This diagram represents Pascal's model of a file that is being written:

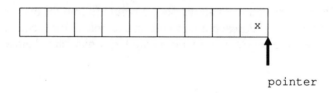

pointer

The boxes represent the components of the file. They must all be of the same type - just like with an array, but as we have seen, there are important differences between arrays and serial files. The pointer points to the place at which the next component will be added to the file. It is moved along by one every time a component is written to the file. In the diagram, the component marked "x" is the one that was most recently added to the file.

162

This diagram represents Pascal's model of a file that is being read:

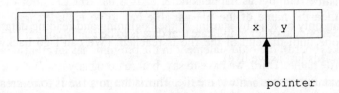

pointer

The component marked "x" is the one that had just been read. The one marked "y" will be brought into main memory if the file is read again.

## Components

The components of the file can be integers, reals, or characters; but all the components of a file must be of the same type. An important restriction is that a file can only be read in the same manner as that in which it was written. For example, if a program creates a file as a file of integers, then all all other programs must read it as a file of integers. Similarly, if a file is created as a file of characters, then other programs cannot read it in any other manner.

Let us begin with a program to display the contents of a file of integers. The algorithm is:

```
while not end of file do
      read some data from file
      write the data to screen
endwhile
```

Here it is in Pascal:

```
program displayFile (input, output, inputData) ;
var
      number    : integer;
      inputData : file of integer ;
begin
reset (inputData) ;
while not eof (inputData) do begin
      read (inputData, number) ;
      write (number) ;
      writeln end
end.
```

Note the following four points about the program. First, the file "inputData" is declared just like a variable, which it is. In addition, if the file exists before the program starts running, as happens here; or if it has to exist after the program finishes, then the name of the file variable has to be included in the program heading. Second, in order to indicate that data is to be read from a file (rather than from the keyboard), the *read* statement in the program has an additional variable in it - the file name. Third, we have to say, before doing any *read* or *write*, that we wish to read, rather than write to the file. That is the purpose of the *reset* statement. Lastly, the thing called "eof" can be tested, as shown, to see if the end of file has been reached. *Eof* becomes true as soon as the last component has been read (or is immediately true if the file is empty).

Now suppose we want to store some information in a new file. The algorithm is:

```
while more information do
      read information from keyboard
      write the information to the file
endwhile
```

Here is the Pascal code for it:

```
program createFile (input, output, outputData) ;
var
      character  : char ;
      outputData : file of char ;
begin
rewrite (outputData) ;
read (character) ;
while character <> '*' do begin
      write (outputData, character) ;
      read (character) end
end.
```

The *rewrite* statement announces our intention of creating a new file. If the file already exists, execution of a *rewrite* causes obliteration of the entire existing contents of the file. Notice that, because there is no file name specified in them, the *read* statements in the program operate on data typed at the keyboard.

# Text files

There is another kind of file in Pascal - the *text* file. It is identical to a file of characters, apart from three important differences:

1.  *Readln, writeln* and *eoln* can be used on text files.

2.  Data in text files can be read into integer, real or character variables.

3.  Data can be written to text files from integer, real or character variables.

These three features make text files the exact backing-store equivalent of the vdu keyboard and screen. In addition, most text editors create files that are text files, so using an editor provides an easier method of creating a data file compared with writing a program to create the file. Text files are usually the most useful kind of file to use with Pascal.

As an example, here is an earlier program modified to use a text file:

```
program cornflakes2 (input, output, inputData) ;
var
      command          : char ;
      quantity, total  : integer ;
      inputData        : text ;
begin
reset (inputData) ;
total := 0 ;
while not eof (inputData) do begin
      read (inputData, quantity) ;
      if command = 'i' then begin
          total := total - quantity end
      else begin
           total := total + quantity end ;
      readln (inputData) ;
      read (inputData, command) end ;
write ('You have ', total, ' boxes')
end.
```

Take note of how the reserved word *text* is used in the declaration of the file. Also, notice that the name of the file has to be specified with *eof* and *readln*.

In Pascal, *input* and *output* are the names for the streams of characters coming from the vdu keyboard and going to the vdu screen. Both input and output are text files, which means that they can easily be passed as parameters to procedures. For instance, we can modify the readWord procedure from chapter 14 to work on either the keyboard or a file by adding a new formal parameter and referring to the new parameter in the *read* statements. Like this:

```
Procedure readWord (var fileName : text ; var word : .......
-
read (fileName, singleChar) ;
-
```

To read a name from the keyboard, we would call readWord like this:

```
readWord (input, name) ;
```

To read a name from a file, we would call readWord like this:

```
readWord (dataFile, name) ;
```

Let us now go on to selectively extract and display information from a file. Suppose a file holds people's names, along with their bank balances. The algorithm for a program to display the names of people who are overdrawn is:

```
while not eof do
      read name
      read balance
      if balance < 0 then
            display details
      endif
endwhile
```

Finally, suppose we want to update the information in a file. For example, suppose £200 is to be added to Doug's account. Remembering that the only way to change a file is to make a copy, the algorithm is:

```
while not end of old file do
      read name
      read balance
      if name is Doug then
            balance := balance + £200
      endif
      write name
      write balance
endwhile
```

# Files as parameters

There is a slight difficulty if we need to use files other than *text* files as procedure parameters. This procedure heading is alright:

```
procedure example1 (var param : text) ;
```

but this one is not allowed by the Pascal grammar:

```
procedure example2 (var param : file of char) ;
```

To get round this problem, we have to use types as explained in the chapter on arrays. The syntax diagrams to use are given at the end of the book.

# Summary

Files are serial in Pascal. They are declared as variables. Before accessing a file, a program must execute either a *reset* or a *rewrite* statement. The *read* and *write* statements are used to access files. We can use *readln*, *writeln*, *eof* and *eoln* with *text* files.

# Exercises

1. Code the above programs which are given merely as designs in pseudo-code. Run them. Hint: the modified readWord procedure will be useful.

2. Develop a program to copy a text file.

3. Develop a program to display a whole file under suitable headings. Write it so that it displays information one page (or screenfull) at a time.

4. Create a personal address and telephone number system. The program should provide the following facilities:
   a. obtain a number, given a name,
   b. change a number, or a name,
   c. enter a new name and number,
   d. delete an entry,
   e. display the entire contents.

5. List the differences between serial files and arrays.

# Epilogue

What can you say that you know, having studied this book? Do you have an understanding of Pascal? The answer is no, because we have only looked at a subset of Pascal. Can you say, then, that you know how to use a computer to develop programs? Well, provided that you have actually got some programs working on a computer, then the answer is yes. But the point is that there is more to programming than using a computer. Do you know how to go about writing programs? Again, provided that you have written the programs suggested, then you have some skill in programming. But be cautious: there is much more to programming than has been described in this book.

This book has tried to explain a *systematic* approach to programming. The most important topic described is the idea of spending time on the *design of a program*.

Perhaps you wonder why Pascal was chosen as the language for learning programming? There are several reasons. First, because it has *if, for* and *while* statements, it facilitates structured programming. Second, Pascal allows data and procedure names to be fairly long. You can also lay out a program just as you like. Both of these features are conducive to clear programming. Finally, Pascal is being used more and more.

There are, of course, things wrong with Pascal. Worst of all - and no doubt you will agree - is the horrible grammar of Pascal, with its semi-colons, *begin*s and *end*s. Second, Pascal has no facility for accessing random access files. Finally, in Pascal, you can't write a program as modules which you can compile separately and later link together.

Why have we looked at only a subset of Pascal in this book? The reason is that we didn't want to get bogged down with all the various facilities of Pascal. Instead we wanted to concentrate on the essentials of good programming without having to worry too much about the programming language.

The most obvious topic not covered in the book is program efficiency. We believe that this is only of secondary importance compared with efficient use of *people's* time. If a clear, understandable program turns out to be too slow or too large, there are techniques for making it more efficient. On the other hand, if a super-efficient program turns out to be incomprehensible, then there is little that can be done about it.

# Bibliography

The following book looks at programming in a similar way to this book.

"Simple Pascal" McGregor J J and Watt A H, Pitman 1981

The major book on top-down stepwise refinement, and on structured programming in general, is as follows. It is not easy reading.

"Structured Programming" Dahl O J, Dijkstra E W, Hoare C A R, Academic Press, London 1972.

There are many good books that give a readable account of the whole of Pascal. An example is:

"Learning to Program" Johnston H, Prentice-Hall International, 1985.

The experiment on program testing, described in the chapter on testing, is given in:

"A controlled experiment in program testing and code walkthroughs/inspections" Myers G J, Communications of the ACM, Volume 21, number 9, September 1978.

# Syntax diagrams

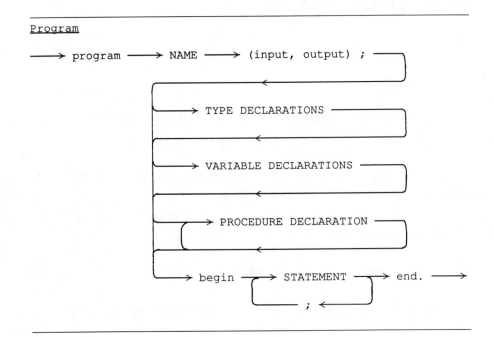

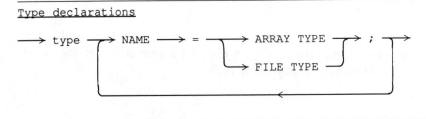

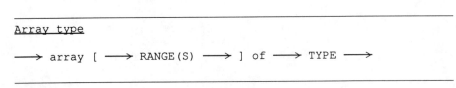

## File type

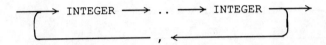

## Range(s)

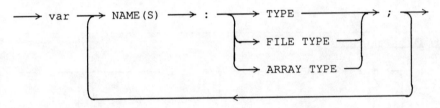

## Variable declarations

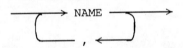

## Name(s)

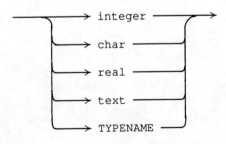

## Type

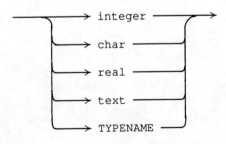

## Procedure declaration

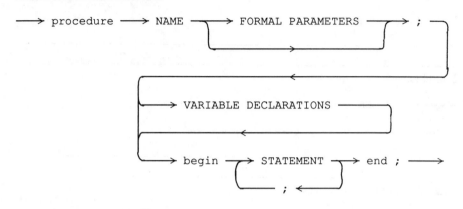

## Formal parameters

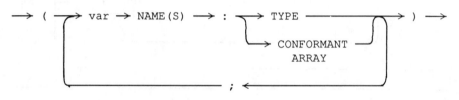

## Conformant array

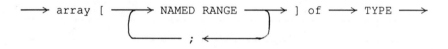

## Named range

## Statement

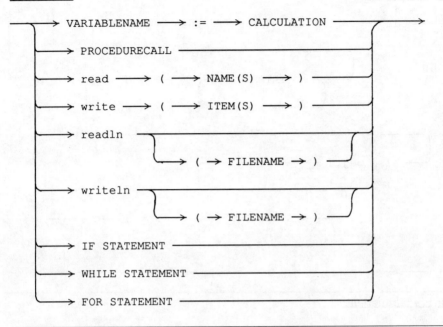

## Item(s)

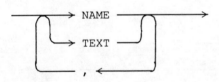

## Procedure call

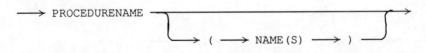

<u>if statement</u>

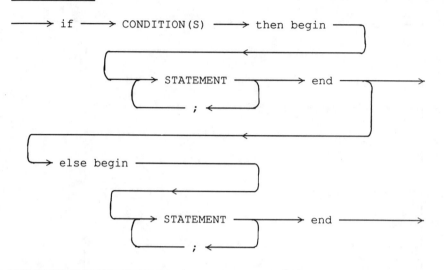

<u>While statement</u>

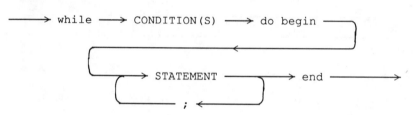

<u>For statement</u>

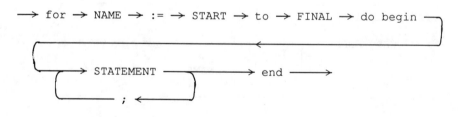

# GENERAL COMPUTING BOOKS

Compiler Physiology for Beginners, M Farmer, 279pp, ISBN 0-86238-064-2
Dictionary of Computer and Information Technology, D Lynch, 225 pages,
ISBN 0-86238-128-2
File Structure and Design, M Cunningham, 211pp, ISBN 0-86238-065-0
Information Technology Dictionary of Acronyms and Abbreviations, D Lynch,
270pp, ISBN 0-86238-153-3
The IBM Personal Computer with BASIC and PC-DOS, B Kynning, 320pp,
ISBN 0-86238-080-4
Project Skills Handbook, S Rogerson, 143pp, ISBN 0-86238-146-0

# PROGRAMMING LANGUAGES

An Intro to LISP, P Smith, 130pp, ISBN 0-86238-187-8
An Intro to OCCAM 2 Programming: 2nd Ed, Bowler, et al, 109pp,
ISBN 0-86238-227-0
C Simply, M Parr, 168pp, ISBN 0-86238-262-9
Cobol for Mainframe and Micro: 2nd Ed, D Watson, 177pp, ISBN 0-86238-211-4
Comparative Languages: 2nd Ed, J R Malone, 125pp, ISBN 0-86238-123-1
Fortran 77 for Non-Scientists, P Adman, 109pp, ISBN 0-86238-074-X
Fortran 77 Solutions to Non-Scientific Problems, P Adman, 150pp,
ISBN 0-86238-087-1
Fortran Lectures at Oxford, F Pettit, 135pp, ISBN 0-86238-122-3
LISP: From Foundations to Applications, G Doukidis et al, 228pp,
ISBN 0-86238-191-6
Programming for Change in Pascal, D Robson, 272pp, ISBN 0-86238-250-5
Prolog versus You, A Johansson, et al, 308pp, ISBN 0-86238-174-6
Simula Begin, G M Birtwistle, et al, 391pp, ISBN 0-86238-009-X
Structured Programming with COBOL & JSP: Vol 1, J B Thompson, 372pp,
ISBN 0-86238-154-1, Vol 2, 354pp, ISBN 0-86238-245-9
The Intensive C Course: 2nd Edition, M Farmer, 186pp, ISBN 0-86238-190-8
The Intensive Pascal Course: 2nd Edition, M Farmer, 125pp, ISBN 0-86238-219-X

# ASSEMBLY LANGUAGE PROGRAMMING

Coding the 68000, N Hellawell, 214pp, ISBN 0-86238-180-0
Computer Organisation and Assembly Language Programming, L Ohlsson & P
Stenstrom, 128pp, ISBN 0-86238-129-0
What is machine code and what can you do with it? N Hellawell, 104pp,
ISBN 0-86238-132-0

# PROGRAMMING TECHNIQUES

Discrete-events simulations models in PASCAL/MT+ on a microcomputer, L P
Jennergren, 135pp, ISBN 0-86238-053-7
Information and Coding, J A Llewellyn, 152pp, ISBN 0-86238-099-5
JSP - A Practical Method of Program Design, L Ingevaldsson, 204pp,
ISBN 0-86238-107-X
Modular Software Design, M Stannett, 136pp, ISBN 0-86238-266-1

Linear Programming: A Computational Approach: 2nd Ed, K K Lau, 150pp,
ISBN 0-86238-182-7
Programming for Beginners: the structured way, D Bell & P Scott, 178pp,
ISBN 0-86238-130-4
Software Engineering for Students, M Coleman & S Pratt, 195pp,
ISBN 0-86238-115-0
Software Taming with Dimensional Design, M Coleman & S Pratt, 164pp,
ISBN 0-86238-142-8
Systems Programming with JSP, B Sanden, 186pp, ISBN 0-86238-054-5

## MATHEMATICS AND COMPUTING

Fourier Transforms in Action, F Pettit, 133pp, ISBN 0-86238-088-X
Generalised Coordinates, L G Chambers, 90pp, ISBN 0-86238-079-0
Statistics and Operations Research, I P Schagen, 300pp, ISBN 0-86238-077-4
Teaching of Modern Engineering Mathematics, L Rade (ed), 225pp,
ISBN 0-86238-173-8
Teaching of Statistics in the Computer Age, L Rade (ed), 248pp, ISBN 0-86238-090-1
The Essentials of Numerical Computation, M Bartholomew-Biggs, 241pp,
ISBN 0-86238-029-4

## DATABASES AND MODELLING

Computer Systems Modelling & Development, D Cornwell, 291pp,
ISBN 0-86238-220-3
An Introduction to Data Structures, B Boffey, D Yates, 250pp, ISBN 0-86238-076-6
Database Analysis and Design: 2nd Ed, H Robinson, 378pp, ISBN 0-86238-018-9
Databases and Database Systems: 2nd Ed, E Oxborrow, 256pp, ISBN 0-86238-091-X
Data Bases and Data Models, B Sundgren, 134pp, ISBN 0-86238-031-6
Text Retrieval and Document Databases, J Ashford & P Willett, 125pp,
ISBN 0-86238-204-1
Information Modelling, J Bubenko (ed), 687pp, ISBN 0-86238-006-5

## UNIX

An Intro to the Unix Operating System, C Duffy, 152pp, ISBN 0-86238-143-6
Operating Systems through Unix, G Emery, 96pp, ISBN 0-86238-086-3

## SYSTEMS ANALYSIS & SYSTEMS DESIGN

Systems Analysis and Development: 3rd Ed, P Layzell & P Loucopoulos, 284pp,
ISBN 0-86238-215-7
SSADM Techniques, Lejk, et al, 350pp, ISBN 0-86238-224-6
Computer Systems: Where Hardware meets Software, C Machin, 200pp,
ISBN 0-86238-075-8
Microcomputer Systems: hardware and software, J Tierney, 168pp,
ISBN 0-86238-218-1
Distributed Applications and Online Dialogues: a design method for application
systems, A Rasmussen, 271pp, ISBN 0-86238-105-3

# HARDWARE

**Computers from First Principles,** M Brown, 128pp, ISBN 0-86238-027-8
**Fundamentals of Microprocessor Systems,** P Witting, 525pp, ISBN 0-86238-030-8

# ELECTRICAL & ELECTRONIC ENGINEERING

**Analogue & Digital Signal Processing & Coding,** P Grant, 450pp,
ISBN 0-86238-206-8
**Handbook of Electronics,** J de Sousa Pires, approx 750pp, ISBN 0-86238-061-8
**Electricity,** T Johansson, 960pp, ISBN 0-86238-208-4
**Interference-free Electronics,** S Benda, ISBN 0-86238-255-6

# NETWORKS

**Communication Network Protocols: 2nd Ed,** B Marsden, 345pp,
ISBN 0-86238-106-1
**Computer Networks: Fundamentals and Practice,** M D Bacon *et al,* 109pp,
ISBN 0-86238-028-6
**Data Networks 1,** Ericsson & Televerket, 250pp, ISBN 0-86238-193-2
**Data Networks 2,** Ericsson & Televerket, 159pp, ISBN 0-86238-221-1
**Telecommunications: Telephone Networks 1,** Ericsson & Televerket, 147pp,
ISBN 0-86238-093-6
**Telecommunications: Telephone Networks 2,** Ericsson & Televerket, 176pp,
ISBN 0-86238-113-4

# GRAPHICS

**An Introductory Course in Computer Graphics,** R Kingslake, 146pp,
ISBN 0-86238-073-1
**Techniques of Interactive Computer Graphics,** A Boyd, 242pp, ISBN 0-86238-024-3
**Two-dimensional Computer Graphics,** S Laflin, 85pp, ISBN 0-86238-127-4

# APPLICATIONS

**Computers in Health and Fitness,** J Abas, 106pp, ISBN 0-86238-155-X
**Developing Expert Systems,** G Doukidis, E Whitley, ISBN 0-86238-196-7
**Expert Systems Introduced,** D Daly, 180pp, ISBN 0-86238-185-1
**Handbook of Finite Element Software,** J Mackerle & B Fredriksson, approx
1000pp, ISBN 0-86238-135-5
***Inside* Data Processing: computers and their effective use in business: 2nd Ed,**
A deWatteville, 150pp, ISBN 0-86238-252-1
**Modelling with Spreadsheets,** A Rothery, 200pp, ISBN 0-86238-258-0
**Proceedings of the Third Scandinavian Conference on Image Analysis,** P
Johansen & P Becker (eds) 426pp, ISBN 0-86238-039-1
**Programmable Control Systems,** G Johannesson, 136pp, ISBN 0-86238-046-4
**Risk and Reliability Appraisal on Microcomputers,** G Singh, with G Kiangi,
142pp, ISBN 0-86238-159-2
**Statistics with Lotus 1-2-3: 2nd Ed,** M Lee & J Soper, 207pp, ISBN 0-86238-244-0

## HCI

**Human/Computer Interaction: from voltage to knowledge,** J Kirakowski, 250pp, ISBN 0-86238-179-7
**Information Ergonomics,** T Ivegard, 228pp, ISBN 0-86238-032-4
**Computer Display Designer's Handbook,** E Wagner, approx 300pp, ISBN 0-86238-171-1

## INFORMATION AND SOCIETY

**Access to Government Records: International Perspectives and Trends,** T Riley, 112pp, ISBN 0-86238-119-3
**CAL/CBT - the great debate,** D Marshall, 300pp, ISBN 0-86238-144-4
**Economic and Trade-Related Aspects of Transborder Dataflow,** R Wellington-Brown, 93pp, ISBN 0-86238-110-X
**Information Technology and a New International Order,** J Becker, 141pp, ISBN 0-86238-043-X
**People or Computers: Three Ways of Looking at Information Systems,** M Nurminen, 1218pp, ISBN 0-86238-184-3
**Transnational Data Flows in the Information Age,** C Hamelink, 115pp, ISBN 0-86238-042-1

## SCIENCE HANDBOOKS

**Alpha Maths Handbook,** L Rade, 199pp, ISBN 0-86238-036-7
**Beta Maths Handbook,** L Rade, 425pp, ISBN 0-86238-140-1
**Nuclear Analytical Chemistry,** D Brune *et al,* 557pp, ISBN 0-86238-047-2
**Physics Handbook,** C Nordling & J Osterman, 430pp, ISBN 0-86238-037-5
**The V-Belt Handbook,** H Palmgren, 287pp, ISBN 0-86238-111-8

Chartwell-Bratt specialise in excellent books at affordable prices.

For further details contact your local bookshop, or ring Chartwell-Bratt direct on **081-467 1956** (Access/Visa welcome.)

Ring or write for our *free* catalogue.

**Chartwell-Bratt (Publishing & Training) Ltd,** Old Orchard, Bickley Road, Bromley, Kent, BR1 2NE, United Kingdom.
Tel 081-467 1956, Fax 081-467 1754

This readable and helpful introduction to Pascal gets you acquainted with the language's major features and develops good programming technique. It emphasises the benefits of spending time on careful program design. The design method of "functional decomposition" – also known as "top-down, step-wise refinement" is explained. The notation used for design throughout the book is a general-purpose pseudo-code.

The reader discovers how to create and list files, run and amend programs, and learns how, in Pascal, integer numbers can be input, calculations done, and output produced. Procedures with local variables and parameters are then introduced. Next, selection and repetition are dealt with, followed by processing character data. A case study in design and coding is followed by chapters on program layout, debugging and testing, systematic working, arrays, real numbers, top-down implementation and file handling. Actual programming practise is given through a variety of exercises.

**Lecturers' comments:**

*"Very well laid out – easy to understand. Excellent!" ... "This is a very good book" ... "Useful comprehensive survey of fundamental concepts" ... "Excellent approach to algorithms" ... "A good introduction to both Pascal and top-down design methods"*

Lecturers from most UK universities are collaborating with Chartwell-Bratt in the preparation of this series of textbooks for computer science students.

Until now there has been a shortage of reasonably priced, up-to-date, and most important, relevant material to support the student, and tutor. This progressive series comprises slim, inexpensive books which individually focus on single key aspects of computer studies, but collectively cover the content of most degree courses, however they are structured. Contact Chartwell-Bratt for details of current and forthcoming titles in the CB Series.

**Chartwell-Bratt Ltd**
Old Orchard, Bickley Road,
Bromley, Kent BR1 2NE,
United Kingdom

ISBN 0-86238-368-4

9 780862 383688

**A CHARTWELL-BRATT
STUDENT TEXT**

# Pascal Simply

## An introduction to Pascal Programming

**Doug Bell  Peter Scott**

Chartwell-Bratt